DEMANDING LIBERTY

An UNTOLD STORY of AMERICAN RELIGIOUS FREEDOM

BRANDON J. O'BRIEN

An imprint of InterVarsity Press
Downers Grove, Illinois

InterVarsity Press
P.O. Box 1400, Downers Grove, IL 60515-1426
ivpress.com
email@ivpress.com

InterVarsity Press® is the book-publishing division of InterVarsity Christian Fellowship/USA®, a movement of students and faculty active on campus at hundreds of universities, colleges, and schools of nursing in the United States of America, and a member movement of the International Fellowship of Evangelical Students. For information about local and regional activities, visit intervarsity.org.

All Scripture quotations, unless otherwise indicated, are taken from the King James Version (KJV). Public domain.

Cover design: David Fassett
Interior design: Daniel van Loon
Images: water: © borchee / iStockphoto / Getty Images
horse: © nicoolay / iStock / Getty Images
Isaac Backus: © Granger Historical Picture Archive / Alamy Stock Photo

ISBN 978-0-8308-4528-6 (print)
ISBN 978-0-8308-8772-9 (digital)

Printed in the United States of America ♾

InterVarsity Press is committed to ecological stewardship and to the conservation of natural resources in all our operations. This book was printed using sustainably sourced paper.

Library of Congress Cataloging-in-Publication Data

A catalog record for this book is available from the Library of Congress.

P *25 24 23 22 21 20 19 18 17 16 15 14 13 12 11 10 9 8 7 6 5 4 3 2 1*
Y *37 36 35 34 33 32 31 30 29 28 27 26 25 24 23 22 21 20 19 18*

And as the present contests about liberty and government are very great, they call loudly for all the light therein that can be gained from every quarter.

Isaac Backus, preface to *A History of New-England*

CONTENTS

INTRODUCTION

Nothing teaches like experience; and what is true history but the experience of those who have gone before us?

ISAAC BACKUS, *A HISTORY OF NEW-ENGLAND*

Imagine how different life would be if Thomas Jefferson had won with his vision for religious liberty in America. There would be no tax exemption for clergy, no federal grants or scholarships for students attending Christian colleges, no federally funded chaplains in the armed forces, no national day of prayer, no claim on our currency that "in God we trust." That great founding father Jefferson believed religious institutions should stand or fall on the merits of their beliefs and not be propped up by the government. He assumed that without the support of the government religious institutions were bound to fall and that the American people would slowly but surely abandon religion altogether. In the meantime, he was sure churches should receive no help from civil powers. None at all. There should stand between the church and state a "wall of separation" that keeps both from meddling in the other's business.

Jefferson's goal was to protect the government from the abuses of religion; thus he believed faith should have no place in government, no weight in legislative decisions, no official public influence at all. Faith could and should be held privately. It could and should promote good citizenship and morality. Church and state as institutions, like neighbors separated by a good fence, could coexist side by side. But they should not collude or cooperate.

Jefferson was not the only man of his generation with a clear vision for the nation's future. New England's Congregationalists, for example, had a competing view of church-and-state relations in the years leading up to America's founding. They fought just as hard as Jefferson to see it come to pass.

Just imagine if *they* had won with *their* vision of religious liberty.

Descended from the Puritans who settled the Massachusetts Bay Colony, New England Congregationalists believed that a nation could thrive only under the direct supervision of God. That supervision should be ensured by Christian magistrates who enforced not only the "second table" of the Ten Commandments —the ones that prohibited murder and theft and the like; but also the "first table"—the ones that commanded keeping the sabbath and worshiping God properly. New England's Congregationalists wanted the freedom to believe and worship like Congregationalists. Everyone else—Baptists and Methodists and Quakers and Catholics—were expected to conform. If the

Congregationalists had gotten their way, *all* of America's citizens would be required by law to attend (authorized) church services regularly, refrain from work on Sunday, and pay special taxes to fund the local Congregational minister, whether you attended his church or not.

This thought experiment wouldn't have made any sense to me a few years ago. For all of my childhood and at least through college, I assumed there was only one view of religious liberty in America that everyone shared, at least from the early years down to about the 1960s. I believed it was this view (this view everyone shared) that was codified in our founding documents, and that the reason the Constitution was ratified and the First Amendment was adopted is because everyone agreed with their contents. As I understood it, there was a "long-standing American tradition of accommodating religious practice and expression that predates the ratification of the Constitution." That tradition may be under attack today. But as far as I knew, it was a universally held and consistently applied tradition.

The experiences of Isaac Backus—the story told in these pages—radically altered my perception of this part of American history. First, I was surprised to discover there was such debate about this value Americans today consider a fundamental ingredient of the American DNA. It was news to me to discover there was no consensus about the relationship between church and state before the American Revolution. Some didn't believe church and state should be separated. Those who believed they should be separated disagreed about why.

Next, it surprised me to learn that this person I'd never heard of—Isaac Backus—had "set forth the principles of separation of Church and State which were to predominate in American life until very recently." This doesn't mean that he created the system we have today. Rather he represented a significant stream of thought that originated a generation or so before him but matured and flourished after his death. Instead of a theocracy, where a church maintained both spiritual and public order, on the one hand, and in place of Jefferson's wall of separation, on the other, Isaac Backus advocated for a "sweet harmony" between church and state. In terms of legislation, America adopted a vision for church-state relations much more similar to Backus's than to Jefferson's or that of the Congregationalists. Of course, Backus didn't win this victory on his own. He was one of many laborers in the field. But Backus played a special role in the movement, and his experience as part of a marginalized religious community in America ran counter to the narrative Americans tell about our consistent commitment to religious liberty. Just imagine that a man I'd never heard of played a significant role in securing religious liberty—a freedom I previously believed America had always protected.

A Case for Isaac Backus

Isaac Backus is a captivating character who lived in a remarkable age. He was a Baptist pastor from rural Connecticut with no formal education who squared off bravely and successfully against both the political and spiritual elites of his day. He played a role in all the major episodes of early American history. Sometimes he played a bit part, sometimes the lead. He became a born-again Christian during the First Great Awakening. He became a Baptist a decade later and quickly rose to prominence among Baptists, helping the movement grow from a handful of loosely affiliated networks in the eighteenth century to one of the nation's largest denominations by the twentieth century. He pastored churches, and soldiers, through the American Revolution. He advocated for religious liberty at the Continental Congress and drafted a Bill of Rights for the American Constitution long before one was officially adopted. He contributed to the early stirrings of the Second Great Awakening. He fought for more than half a century to make America a nation that protects every citizen's right to exercise their religion according to their conscience.

As I see it, all those things make Backus interesting; they also make him *useful*. Backus lived in a generation of transition. When he was *born* in Connecticut, it was an English colony; when he *died*, Connecticut was one of the United States. He was born a royal subject and died an American citizen. His was an age of religious revival and, at the same time, growing secularism. In his lifetime, powerful men debated the limits of liberty, the role of the government, and the future of a nation.

Whether or not we are living in a generation of transition ourselves is hard to say with certainty. Historians will decide that in the future. Even so, it certainly feels like things are changing. There is a host of religious and political commentators heralding tectonic shifts in the present generation. If they're right, what do we do? To answer that question for the future, we would do well to examine our past. Backus made the case for the value of history this way: "Nothing teaches like experience," he wrote. "And what is true history but the experience of those who have gone before us?" Backus's experience in a generation of change may have something helpful to teach us.

Backus's experience already has proven helpful to me personally. Backus's faith journey, for example, helped me make sense of my own. The Christian tradition I was raised in was generous and gracious—it taught me to love Jesus, and for that I'll be grateful always. Nevertheless, on a number of subjects this tradition created some confusion for me about the nature of our shared faith. If the only thing you had to judge by was our events calendar, you might assume that our two most important holidays were Christmas and the Fourth of July. Those were the two times of year we did it up right in worship, really pulled out all the stops. Those were the two times of year we made a focused effort to reach out to the community. We did so at Christmas through a large-scale musical production aimed at attracting non-Christians and reminding them (or informing them) what the X in Xmas stands for. Around Independence Day we targeted the community with a full-choir concert of patriotic songs on the steps of city hall.

This was the American South in the 1980s and 1990s. Our faith was shot through with patriotism and our patriotism shot through with faith. I didn't realize this until college, but it became clear to me in my sophomore year, when I roomed with an Austrian student named Sammy. The exact details of this story escape me now, but the salient parts are these: we attended a church service together one Sunday, and when we returned to our room, Sammy expressed deep concern about some of the religious symbolism in the sanctuary. Most of what he saw was what he expected—a baptistery, an empty cross, a Communion table. What caught him by surprise was the presence of a flag. He couldn't understand why there would be an American flag in a house of worship. I couldn't understand why there shouldn't be. *Wasn't a national flag in a house of worship evidence of unfaithful collusion between church and state?* he wondered. It's a fair question from someone raised in a country with a living memory of Nazism. It turns out patriotic symbolism is not an essential part of Christian worship everywhere on the globe. That was news to me.

Experiences like these in college set me on a journey to distinguish the parts of my faith that were essentially and universally Christian from those parts that were culturally conditioned by my context in America. One result of that journey was a book I coauthored with Randy Richards, *Misreading Scripture with Western Eyes*. In that book, we identify ways our Western-ness, including our American-ness, affects the way we interpret the Bible. The book remains an important milestone in my journey, and I'm continually grateful to Randy for including me in the project.

But no one book can address all the questions. I had questions about culture and politics and social issues and any number of other issues. To bring the conversation back around to the topic of this book, for years I'd puzzled over questions such as, Why do so many Christians I know insist that America was founded on Christian principles and yet vehemently insist that the state has no right to meddle in church affairs? Why do so many Christians I know celebrate the religious liberties America protects and yet support federal initiatives to limit the liberties of certain religious groups? Why do so many Christians I know champion the separation of church and state and yet seem to expect the government to support Christian activities through tax exemption and other forms of subsidy?

In this journey to crack the shell of American Christianity and find the kernel of true faith inside, Isaac Backus was the first reliable guide from history that I encountered. I think it's because he spoke my language. He was a Baptist, as I was at the beginning of my journey and like the people who brought me up in the faith. He was a product of revival, just as I was. And while his populism and mine had different sources and histories, he felt like a man of the people. He was thoughtful, but he wasn't a theorist. He was a pastor, and all his writings bear the stamp of someone who is concerned with how the subject at hand should apply in a normal person's life. Backus was an armchair historian and theologian, a keen observer of human nature. He was, in contemporary terms, an activist. He fought "the Man" and won, albeit several years after he died.

All this made him the kind of man other people looked to for guidance in his own day too. "Few men have more uniformly lived and acted up to" the high calling of a Christian minister, said one of his friends. "He was a burning and shining light," this friend went on. "In both praying and preaching, he often appeared to be favored with such a degree of divine unction, as to render it manifest to all that God was with him."

Truly a man for all seasons, Backus has helped me think through some of the issues of our day by forcing me to think through with him the issues he faced in his. And, as will become clearer in a moment, he introduced me to a whole world of thought on the subject of religious liberty specifically.

Of course, Backus wasn't always right. His opponents certainly didn't think he was. Some of his educated detractors considered him ignorant and unqualified, just a "young upstart, not to be regarded," an uneducated "gumphead." Others viewed him as worse than ignorant, a "crafty deceiver" whose ideas threatened to undermine the social fabric. Both of these assessments are unfair, in my opinion. But the fact remains that, like all of us, Backus was conditioned by his times and blind to certain things. Where he's right, I've found him to be a helpful guide whose example can suggest a way over the uncertain terrain we face. Where he's wrong, his errors and assumptions have helped me uncover and give attention to my own mistakes and misperceptions.

If he was nothing else, Isaac Backus was a tireless advocate for religious liberty for almost his entire adult life. That alone would make his story worth telling. But the fact that Backus *had to fight* for religious liberty, the fact that for more than half a century he labored within a much-maligned and often-persecuted religious minority, tells us something important about the America Backus lived and died in. It was not a forgone conclusion before 1800 that the religious practices of all Americans should be equally protected under the law.

It's helpful to remember from the very beginning of this story that the citizens of this continent have debated what religious liberty means and what freedoms should be protected since before the English colonies became the United States. Based on our experience in the twenty-first century, it may seem that America has never been more divided over religious issues. The Pew Research Center reported in late 2016 that the American public was almost evenly divided on the question of whether "wedding-related businesses, such as caterers and florists, should be required to serve same-sex couples who want to marry, even if the owner of these establishments objects to homosexuality for religious reasons." Nearly fifty-fifty.

It can be tempting to read a statistic like that as evidence of decline from a previous age, when most people essentially agreed about what basic religious liberty entails. Professional historians will have a more textured and nuanced understanding of America's history than that. But in my experience, the average American—more specifically, the average evangelical American—tends to assume that there was a golden age of religious liberty sometime in the past, and we have been in decline since the 1960s or so.

If Isaac Backus were alive today, he would feel the need to correct the misperception that there was ever a "long-standing American tradition of accommodating religious practice and expression" in the years before or even *after* the Constitution was ratified. He might tell us about the time his mother was arrested for refusing to pay religious taxes. He might tell us about the time a congregation of New England Baptists had their property seized and their orchards destroyed for holding unauthorized worship services. He would almost certainly tell us about the time he debated with John and Samuel Adams about how *claiming* to defend religious liberty was not enough. The laws had to be *enforced* if they were to matter at all.

Some Obligatory Apologies About This Book

Writing this story has been difficult for several reasons.

For one, the story is enormous and complicated. We could cover this material by zeroing in on political history or theology or economics. (*I* couldn't. But *someone* could.) We could include sociological research on the differences in daily life and mores between the thirteen original colonies. Volumes have been written—and this could have been another one—on *each* of the episodes in Backus's story: the First Great Awakening, the American Revolution, and the Second Great Awakening, to name a few.

Perhaps the greater difficulty for me is that I've found this story, and this man, enlightening and helpful. This story *means* something to me. It's personal. That reality makes it hard for me to tell this story without inserting myself into it—and trying to pull you into it too.

Decisions have to be made. You can't include everything. So here are a few words to say, as concretely as I can, what this book is *not*. It is not a comprehensive survey of all the views of religious liberty in currency in the eighteenth century. It is not a detailed assessment of the differences between the concepts "separation of church and state" and "religious liberty" and "liberty of conscience." It is not, strictly speaking, a biography. Isaac Backus deserves a good, scholarly biography and this is not it. In fact, this book is not exhaustive in any sense, except that there is more in here about Isaac Backus's argument for religious liberty than you will find nearly anywhere else. The goal of this book is not to make a unique historical contribution, but there are places that it does.

Instead, my goal has been to tell the story of the life and work of Isaac Backus in a way that emphasizes the most challenging or applicable details for today. Backus's long experience of religious persecution in America will surprise many readers, so I've emphasized it. It's useful too for helping American Christians imagine what it might look like to live faithfully as a marginalized community in our own America.

The approach I've chosen for this book assumes a certain kind of reader. This book is for people who care about the issues surrounding religious liberty today, and believe, as I do, that some historical perspective can help us consider our current situation from a new angle. It is for people who fear things are worse now than they ever have been, that our rights are more violated or that freedom is more fragile, and they need courage to face the future. It is for people who crave a theological framework for understanding religious liberty. They will not find answers to all their questions here, but they can begin the journey here. I'm assuming that you, reader, are a thoughtful and intelligent person who is not an expert in American history or religious liberty. My goal is to introduce you to this fascinating person, Isaac Backus, and his extraordinary work. I hope his story inspires you to engage the world today in new and creative ways.

In other words, this book is as much about today as it is about the past. It tells the story of the life and work of Isaac Backus, an important figure I think more Christians ought to know about. At key points in Backus's story, I draw connections to the present. Most of the time, I describe how some part of Backus's story or another affected me, shaped my thinking, adjusted my posture, and so forth. I am not qualified to tell you how to apply this historical narrative to your own life. That will be your job. You'll be frustrated with me about this at some point. That's fine. Because ultimately my goal is to encourage reflection on the past that results in reflection about the present.

The title of the book—*Demanding Liberty*—alludes to this goal. There are two ways to read the title. *Demanding* can be a verb, in the sense that Isaac Backus spent more than half a century *demanding* liberty. *Demanding* can also be an adjective, in the sense that those who enjoy a greater measure of liberty than Backus and others did must steward our liberty well. Doing so is *demanding*.

—∞—

If Backus were here to witness the "great present contests about liberty and government" that occupy our newsfeeds today, I suspect he might say, "We've been here before." There is nothing new under the sun. Liberty has always been an ideal toward which America has reached imperfectly. Backus himself believed there was a golden age of liberty in America. It ended in the eighteenth century, before America became a nation. In the years leading up to independence, Americans considered some religious ideas too dangerous to tolerate and banned them—ideas held by Catholics, Quakers, and my spiritual ancestors, Baptists.

The past has a lot to teach us.

ONE

"FILLED UP WITH SIN"

WHY AMERICA NEEDED A REVIVAL

My soul yielded all into His hands, fell at His feet, and was silent and calm before Him. . . . My heavy burden was gone, tormenting fears were fled, and my joy was unspeakable.

Isaac Backus's account of his conversion

It's nearly impossible for me to imagine colonial New England without a religious image springing to mind. I start thinking about the English settlers who journeyed to the New World to pioneer a new life, and soon my head is filled with images of Pilgrims in black buckled hats giving thanks to God for the bounty of a new world. If it's not the Pilgrims, it's someone like John Winthrop, rocking gently on the good ship Arbella and articulating his ambition that he and his fellow settlers will be a "city on a hill" in the new wilderness of testing. Even when the mental image of the colonial era is negative, it is often religious—

like the dark, dour Puritans of Nathaniel Hawthorne's "Young Goodman Brown" and other stories. Google "colonial America" and the first few pictures that appear depict people preaching or praying.

These images can overstate the piety of the first American colonists. The truth is the colonies were unevenly devout. Faith was arguably a more fundamental aspect of life in New England than it was in some Southern colonies. In New England, villages were often constructed with a church, or "meetinghouse," at the center, and the rest of civilization radiating from it like spokes on a wheel. But just because the meetinghouse was the central feature of the New England village doesn't mean the Christian faith was the driving beat of every citizen's heart. America before the Revolution was not as religious as many imagine.

The first generation of New Englanders, those who colonized Plymouth beginning in 1620 and who established Massachusetts Bay Colony beginning in 1630, had a clear sense of their calling and purpose in the New World and had made the journey to America at great personal cost and risk. But religious commitment is difficult to transmit from one generation to the next. Already by the second generation many lamented the decline of the people's commitment to God and to the founding vision of the Christian commonwealth.

Benjamin Tompson's 1676 poem "New England's Crisis" gives some idea of the kinds of changes the older faithful found troubling. The subtitle sets the tone. His poem told the tale "Of New England's Lamentable Estate at Present, Compared with the

Former (but Few) Years of Prosperity." Tompson reminisces (in meter) about an age when people were happy as songbirds with simple diets and modest clothes—"When flesh was food and hairy skins made coats / And men as well as birds had chirping notes." In his generation, backbiting and gossip were common. The earlier golden years, by contrast, were made up of days "When honest sisters met to pray not prate / About their own and not their neighbor's state."

Alas, these "golden times (too fortunate to hold) / Were quickly signed away for love of gold." The modest fashion of New England's founding fathers was gradually replaced by new trends from Europe. No longer satisfied with a simple diet, the colony began importing chocolate and French wine and exotic fruits. People couldn't delay gratifying their new and sophisticated palates long enough to pray over their meal. They were unkind to one another on the streets. Materially, the colony experienced a season of prosperity. Spiritually, in Tompson's view, the colony was increasingly impoverished. Tompson grieved the loss of simpler times, when "New England's beauties, which still seemed to me / Illustrious in their own simplicity."

Growing materialism was an external symptom, men like Tompson believed, of New England's internal spiritual problems. The children of churchgoers showed little interest in their parents' faith. A series of debates about baptism and the Lord's Supper divided Christians. Frequent bloody conflicts with Native Americans led many leaders in the 1660s and beyond to believe God was punishing his people for their disobedience. The

Puritans, those pioneers who established Massachusetts Bay Colony (which ultimately absorbed Plymouth Plantation), believed they were in a special covenant with God. Keeping that covenant was a group effort. And now, because the group was failing just a generation after the covenant was forged, it was showing signs of breaking.

Pastors developed a style of sermon called the "jeremiad" as a response to spiritual decline. The format gets its name from the biblical "weeping prophet," Jeremiah, who lamented the sins of his people Israel and warned them of God's impending judgment. Many New England preachers, who considered New Englanders a new Israel, took up the same task and called the populace to repentance.

In some places, congregations got the message and repented. Over the next seventy or eighty years, seasons of spiritual renewal and rededication known as "awakenings" became a common feature of the New England religious experience. One type of revival service was the covenant renewal service, which started becoming popular in the 1670s. These were essentially seasons in which pastors reminded their congregations of their duties to God and each other. The events gave church members opportunity to assess their personal relationship with God and provided an opportunity for people who were considering joining the church to convert and become full members. During covenant renewal seasons, preaching focused on salvation, and conversions were frequent. As a result of these events, congregations here and there experienced seasons of spiritual revival.

But a wholesale, wide-scale return to holiness remained out of reach. Church attendance remained low. Roger Finke and Rodney Stark have estimated that in 1776, only 17 percent of American colonists were religiously affiliated. That number must have been even lower the generation before. A meetinghouse may have sat in the center of town, but some villages boasted more taverns than churches. In the first half of the eighteenth century, young people were postponing marriage until their late twenties. The result was a "well-developed youth culture" that brought a range of sins—from simple idleness and disrespect to sexual immorality. Roughly a third of babies in New England were conceived out of wedlock. Religious leaders committed to a vision of a Christian commonwealth in the New World saw that vision evaporating. Their society was losing its moorings, and New England was becoming less faithful. For decades many Christians prayed for an act of God to rekindle the spiritual life of New England.

In the 1740s it appeared to many that their prayers were answered. A generation of backsliders and spiritual sluggards was yanked to its feet by fiery preachers who delivered simple, passionate messages in a new theatrical style in a movement that came to be called the Great Awakening.

The Divine Dramatist

The Great Awakening (sometimes called "the Awakening") had no single champion or representative, but it did have one singular luminary. No revival preacher at the time had more influence than George Whitefield. He was a superstar, America's first celebrity. Imagine Beatlemania or Bieber Fever in an age of periwigs and petticoats.

In the mid-1700s, Whitefield traveled from England to America thirteen times and logged some eighty thousand miles crisscrossing the colonies. Benjamin Franklin, the famous newspaperman from Philadelphia, was a contemporary of Whitefield's and a committed agnostic. He didn't believe a word Whitefield said when he preached the gospel, but Franklin couldn't help but admire him. In fact, the two were good friends, and Franklin attended many of Whitefield's events. Whitefield's speaking style was so refined, Franklin wrote, "that every accent, every emphasis, every modulation of voice, was so perfectly well turned and well placed," that even if you had no interest in the subject matter—and Franklin didn't—"one could not help being pleased with the discourse." It elicited the same sort of pleasure as listening to "an excellent piece of music." This was quite a change of pace from the average sermon of the day, which was typically read aloud by a seated pastor in some degree of monotone. Whitefield was captivating. Rumor has it he could cause a crowd to swoon by the way he pronounced the word *Mesopotamia*.

At one event, Franklin did the math and estimated Whitefield could preach to more than 30,000 people in the open air, without amplification. "He had a loud and clear voice," Franklin observed, "and articulated his words and sentences so perfectly that he might be heard and understood at a great distance." It helped that his audience, "however numerous, observed the most exact silence." But the immensity of Whitefield's audiences testifies to more than the power of his voice. It testifies, too, to his extraordinary appeal in colonial America. Boston was America's most populous city in 1740. In that year, the entire population of Boston was around 16,400 souls. A crowd of 30,000 would have been equivalent to the entire populations of Boston and Philadelphia at the time.

Wherever Whitefield preached, people swarmed from cities and villages to hear him. A New England farmer, Nathan Cole, recorded in his journal his experience of hearing Whitefield preach. Cole knew Whitefield by reputation and "longed to see and hear him, and wished he would come this way." Soon enough, he had his chance:

> Then on a Sudden, in the morning about 8 or 9 of the Clock there came a messenger and said Mr. Whitefield preached at Hartford and Wethersfield yesterday and is to preach at Middletown this morning at ten of the Clock. I was in my field at Work, I dropt my tool I had in my hand and ran home to my wife telling her to make ready quickly to go and hear Mr. Whitefield preach at Middletown, then run to my pasture for my horse with all my might; fearing that I should be too late; having my horse I with my wife soon mounted the horse and went forward as fast as I thought the horse could bear, and when my horse got much out of breath I would get down and put my wife on

> the Saddle and bid her ride as fast as she could and not stop or slack for me except I bade her and so I would run until I was much out of breath; and then mount my horse again, and so I did several times to favor my horse; we improved every moment to get along as if we were fleeing for our lives; all the while fearing we should be too late to hear the sermon.

It's difficult to imagine this level of enthusiasm about a sermon from any preacher in modern times. In the years before digital streaming entertainment, this was about as good as it got.

Cole and his wife were not the only ones frantic to hear Whitefield preach. They soon ran into traffic in their breakneck journey to see the English celebrity:

> And when we came within about half a mile or a mile of the road that comes down from Hartford, Wethersfield and Stepney to Middletown; on high land I saw before me a cloud or fog rising; I first thought it came from the great River, but I came near the road, I heard a noise something like a low rumbling thunder and presently found it was the noise of horses feet coming down the road and this cloud was a cloud of dust made by the horses feet; it arose some rods into the air over the tops of hills and trees and when I came within about 20 rods of the road, I could see men and horses slipping along in the cloud like shadows and as I drew nearer it seemed like a steady stream of horses and their riders, scarcely a horse more than a length behind

> another, all of a lather and foam with sweat, their breath rolling out of their nostrils every Jump; every horse seemed to go with all his might to carry his rider to hear news from heaven for the saving of souls; it made me tremble to see the sight.

The sermon the Coles heard that day touched on the themes Whitefield included in most of his sermons. Whitefield was no feel-good preacher. Cole said of the sermon,

> And my hearing him preach gave me a heart wound; by God's blessing my old foundation was broken up, and I saw that my righteousness would not save me; then I was convinced of the doctrine of Election and went right to quarrelling with God about it, because all that I could do would not save me; and he had decreed from Eternity who should be saved and who not.

Like other revival preachers at the time, Whitefield assured his listeners that they were wretched sinners doomed for the fires of hell. Franklin marveled at the fact that people traveled so far only to hear a preacher describe them all as "naturally half beasts and half devils." Nevertheless, the message about human depravity and God's grace struck a chord in the colonies. Sinners heard again and again—not just from Whitefield but from a host of other preachers—that they must repent of their sins and have a personal and converting experience of faith. If they did, they could experience the "new birth" and be "born again."

The Awakening drew a line in the sand and demanded that a casual, inherited faith was no faith at all. People responded, and the effects of their new birth, in some towns, were palpable in society. Franklin saw the transformation too, although he doubted there was anything supernatural about it. "From being thoughtless or indifferent about religion," Franklin observed, "it seemed as if all the world were growing religious, so that one could not walk through the town in an evening without hearing psalms sung in different families of every street."

Other Luminaries

George Whitefield was not the only important figure of the Awakening. There were the Wesley brothers, John and Charles, whose followers became known as Methodists. In addition to writing hymns still sung in churches the world over today, they founded a movement that became America's largest Christian denomination in the following century.

And there was Jonathan Edwards, the reserved and startlingly brilliant pastor whose uncharacteristically grim sermon "Sinners in the Hands of an Angry God" brought white-knuckled Christians to their knees in repentance in more than one parish church. If George Whitefield was the movement's most notable evangelist, Edwards was its most influential theologian. Edwards led his congregation in Northampton, Massachusetts, through a season of awakening in the early 1730s, at which time nearly three hundred people converted and joined the church. Three hundred people is a lot of people, until we put the number in perspective. Then it becomes a *whole* lot of people. The average church in Edwards's day usually had about seventy-five in attendance. It's possible the Awakening more than quadrupled the size of Edwards's congregation.

Edwards wrote an account of these events called *A Faithful Narrative of the Surprising Work of God*. What made Edwards unique is that he was a diligent student of the Enlightenment's most important rationalistic writings, which were increasingly en vogue in America at the time. *A Faithful Narrative* is a personal testimony of God's work in people's lives written as if it were the scientific observations of a trained botanist or zoologist. He carefully recorded and cataloged the events of the Awakening, including excesses and abuses, to help people know how to recognize the work of the Holy Spirit when they saw it.

A Faithful Narrative was published in England in 1737. When it appeared in print, it influenced important British evangelicals, including Isaac Watts, John and Charles Wesley, and even George Whitefield, inspiring them to expect and pray for spiritual awakening. Edwards ultimately helped to establish the theological center of the Awakening. He mentored George Whitefield, who took Edwards's carefully reasoned theology and popularized it for tens of thousands in his sermons.

That brings us to Isaac Backus.

Filled Up with Sin

Isaac Backus was profoundly influenced by the work of both George Whitefield and Jonathan Edwards. When Backus presented a case for religious liberty before the First Continental Congress three decades after the Awakening, the heart of his argument borrowed from Edwards's theology. But that's jumping ahead. George Whitefield played a key role in Backus's conversion, even though Backus didn't hear Whitefield preach until several years after he was "born again."

Revival fire burned through Backus's hometown of Norwich, Connecticut, when he was a teenager. Backus's mother, Elizabeth, was caught up in it. When Isaac was fifteen or sixteen, his mother experienced the new birth. She became devout and prayed for her son. But Isaac wasn't impressed. Maybe it was typical teenage rebellion. Maybe it was sincere religious apathy. But Backus resisted. He rarely attended church and didn't care much about the revival smoldering around him.

Backus reflected the spirit of the age, with its rebellious youth culture, in his teenage disregard for religion. He illustrated, too, how a deep concern for faith can skip a generation. Backus's hometown, Norwich, was established in 1660 for religious reasons, when Pastor James Fitch led a majority of his congregants not only to start a new church but indeed to plant a new town. Pastor Fitch and his congregants felt that some new rules about church governance within the Congregational Church, known as the Saybrook Platform, took control of the local church out of the hands of the people. So they left. Among those who left Saybrook to found Norwich was Backus's great-grandfather.

But Backus felt no family pressure to take his faith seriously until the Awakening. Even though he witnessed "powerful preaching" and "the sight of many in distress or joy," Backus remained a "hardened sinner" until August 24, 1741, when God led him to "embrace salvation in His own way." Backus was alone in a field working, as Nathan Cole had been when news of Whitefield's visit reached him. Outside the walls of a church, without the appeal of a preacher, Backus experienced the presence of God:

> As I was mowing in the field alone I was thinking of my case; and all my past life seemed to be brought fresh to my view and it appeared indeed nothing but a life of sin. I felt so that I left work and went and sat down under a shady tree; and I was brought to look particularly into my duties and strivings, how I had tried to mend myself by my tears, prayers, and promises of doing better[—]but all in vain—my heart was hard and full of corruption still. And it appeared clear to me then that I had tried every way that I possibly could and if I perished forever I could do no more. And the justice of God shined so clear before my eyes in condemning such a guilty rebel that I could say no more—but fell at his feet. . . . I felt a calm in my mind—them tossings and tumults that I felt before seemed to be gone.

A couple days later, Backus attended an evening prayer service in which someone read a sermon by George Whitefield on Acts 19:2: "He said unto them, Have ye received the Holy Ghost since ye believed?" In the sermon, Whitefield delineated the evidence of true conversion. Backus did not yet consider himself born again. But as he listened to the sermon he identified "marks of true grace" in his own life: "a spirit of prayer—a loathing and hatred of sin—love to the brethren, etc." In that moment "the Lord was pleased to give me some sweet sealings of the Holy Spirit of promise." For the rest of his life he looked back on that moment as the time he left the darkness and entered the light.

Once he was convinced he was converted, Backus never doubted the work God had done in his life. But he did have questions about what this change meant for him. He was hesitant, for example, to join the local church in town, because the pastor honored a practice called the "Half-Way Covenant." The Half-Way Covenant essentially allowed for people to become members of the church without giving an account of their personal faith or conversion. If they lived a moral life and didn't commit any grievous sins, they could enjoy Communion in the church without being converted. Their children could be baptized in the church, too, and grow up as members.

Like others in town who experienced conversion during the Awakening, Backus felt halfway membership undervalued the personal experience of saving faith. His own experience with saving faith convinced him that true faith can't be inherited. Besides, there is some evidence that the pastor of the Congregational church in town, Benjamin Lord, had opposed the Great Awakening because it encouraged uneducated men to preach unauthorized sermons. For these reasons, Backus waited almost a year before he finally decided to join the church, despite his misgivings. He joined the church with the goal that he and the other born-again members could reform the church's membership policy from the inside. They had enough confidence in the power of God to believe that he could use their example to change the heart of their pastor.

In this instance, God did not change the pastor's heart. In 1744, Backus and his mother, along with several of the most prominent families in town, left the Norwich standing church and formed their own congregation. When they did this, they became known as "Separates," because they had *separated* themselves from the majority of believers in town. The pastor said the reasons weren't good enough and demanded that they come back to church posthaste. Backus refused, and he, his mother, and their close friends were excommunicated.

Backus's pastor, Benjamin Lord, was one of many at the time who refused to believe that the Awakening was the work of God because the movement had too many abuses, too many strange and socially unacceptable consequences. Critics had a point. In addition to the thoughtful and cautious advocates of the Awakening, like Edwards, there were other, more radical advocates. There were book-burning populists who heaped into large piles volumes written by "unregenerate" pastors and theologians and set them on fire. Men such as Theodorus Frelinghuysen and Gilbert Tennent threatened the social order by questioning the faith of local ministers. Tennent, a Scots-Irish Presbyterian, preached an infamous sermon titled "The Danger of an

Unconverted Clergy" (1739), in which he suggested that most of the pastors in most of the churches in New England were not actually born-again Christians. James Davenport, in 1741, decried New Haven's minister as a sheep in wolf's clothing. He itinerated in New England, preaching in the streets against the orders of local ministers and eventually was arrested for slander. In the same year, David Brainerd was expelled from Yale for claiming one tutor had "no more grace than [a] chair."

The Awakening was plagued with other excesses. Some of the awakened claimed to receive special spiritual visions from the Lord. Others experienced uncommon manifestations of the Holy Spirit's presence, including groans, shaking, and "holy laughter." Some went so far as to break down all social barriers, encouraging women, children, and even slaves not only to *experience* the new birth but also to *preach* about it.

Backus would almost certainly have taken issue with most of these excesses—though he probably would have delighted to hear a slave preach the gospel. Nevertheless, these are the people Backus became associated with when he left his church in Norwich.

Thus Backus experienced two conversions during the Awakening. The positive conversion was that he passed from darkness to light, death to life—he experienced the new birth the Awakening emphasized. The negative conversion was that he began his journey toward becoming socially marginalized because of his religious convictions. In this area Backus had something to lose. He had been born into a prominent and conservative family in Norwich in 1724, about sixty years after it was founded. His father, Samuel, had served in the General Assembly. His grandfather had been a justice of the peace. His great-grandfather had been a founding member of the commonwealth. Before the Awakening, Backus was a wealthy farmer, a man of means who enjoyed a privileged status. Whatever he gained spiritually upon his conversion to faith, he also sacrificed a great deal materially and socially. The rest of his life was marked by conflict and the struggle for respectability—a respectability he could have kept as his birthright if he'd said no to God's call to new birth.

Revival and Its Consequences

The Great Awakening had a profound impact on eighteenth-century America. America feels the impact of that revival even now in the twenty-first century. But it is easy to overstate the *immediate* effects of the revival on colonial culture. If Finke and Stark are right that only 17 percent of colonial Americans attended church in 1776—almost thirty years *after* the Awakening—we can assume that the rates of church attendance were lower before the Awakening and that the revivals were responsible for bringing the rates *up to* 17 percent. While the experience of new birth certainly changed individual lives and even some villages dramatically, in many towns—as in Norwich—there were not enough converts to change the polity of the local church, much less the culture of the entire town.

Perhaps the greatest large-scale change the Awakening introduced was shifting the religious balance in America. This is especially true in New England. Fewer than 20 percent of the population attended church regularly, but most of those churchgoers belonged to one denomination. The Congregationalists in New England owned the largest percentage of the religious market share. More than 70 percent of churchgoers in Massachusetts were Congregationalist. Roughly 65 percent were Congregationalist in Backus's home state of Connecticut. That began to change with the Awakening. Over the next hundred years, Congregational churches got a smaller and smaller portion of the churchgoing pie, and newer denominations gobbled up the rest.

This is still only part of the story. Ironically, this Great Awakening took place at a time when a different portion of the American population was becoming *less* religious. As some Americans were becoming convinced that God wanted a personal relationship with them, others were becoming convinced that it was nonsense to believe in a personal God who concerned himself with human affairs. Benjamin Franklin is a great example of this. He experienced his own conversion during the Great Awakening—he became a deist. Franklin and others like him, including Thomas Jefferson, were exchanging traditional faith for something more material and secular and scientific. Beginning around the mid-eighteenth century, then, American culture was pulled in opposite directions—the pietists (those converted during or friendly to the Awakening) pulled it in one direction, and the rationalists (like Franklin) pulled it in the other. Most Americans sat somewhere in the middle.

The point of all this is simply to say that the greatest immediate change the Awakening brought was increased tension among religious people. The more religious life diversified in New England, the more conflict was brought out into the open. Marginal groups, like Baptists and Quakers, had experienced persecution in Puritan New England in the past. In the years to come, the resentment that resulted from the Awakening would lead to increased persecution against religious minorities in New England and beyond. Traditional religion fought battles on at least two fronts: it fought both pietism and rationalism. That means it saw enemies everywhere.

Congregationalists, the descendants of the Puritans who had preached jeremiads and prayed for revival, lost power after the Awakening. Their experiment had always been fragile. Now they saw it unraveling at the seams. A growing number of unsatisfied, insubordinate folks were boldly threatening to dismantle the edifice the "Standing Order" had been building for generations.

This is where religious liberty gets hard—when it feels like a zero-sum game. It's one thing to be tolerant of others when the "others" make up a small minority of the population. But when their numbers begin to grow, their presence becomes a threat. Today, the Pew Religious Landscape Study concludes that more than 70 percent of the American population identifies as a Christian of some variety. A quarter of all Americans are identified as "evangelical Protestant." The percentage of religiously unaffiliated persons is almost 23 percent, just a couple points from the percentage of evangelicals. It's no wonder many evangelical Christians feel insecure or even threatened; the landscape is shifting. The evangelical slice of the pie is shrinking. The question, of course, is, What now?

Backus would soon discover the power of history and leverage it to support his movement. First, though, he would learn that no matter who is right about history, the people in power get to decide what is true.

TWO

MINISTRY AND THE HOLY SPIRIT

Multitudes place their qualifications more in human learning than in divine enlightenment and place their authority more in being externally called and set apart by men, than in being internally called by the Spirit of God.

Isaac Backus, *A Discourse Showing the Nature and Necessity of an Internal Call to Preach the Everlasting Gospel*

When I experienced God calling me into ministry in high school, I felt like I was being conscripted into battle. We referred to answering the call as "surrendering to gospel ministry," so the feeling of being drafted seems justified. Keenly did I feel the promise of ostracism—"the world behind me, the cross before me" and "though none go with me, I still will follow" and all that. I counted the cost and decided the payoff was worth it.

In return for my obedience, I secured a role in taking an errant culture back to Jesus.

People had prayed that the Lord of the harvest would raise up workers to tend the field of ever more secular America. I was one of the chosen. No turning back.

I can't help but think Isaac Backus felt a similar responsibility. There was considerably more at stake in the eighteenth century. For me the marginalization and opposition I feared was largely psychological. I wouldn't fit in. In the eighteenth century, answering the call to ministry without going through the proper channels could make you a criminal.

Old Lights, New Lights, and Separates

The Great Awakening brought lasting spiritual renewal to many in the American colonies. But instead of resulting in a unified or homogenous religious landscape, the revivals initiated changes that resulted in a wide range of new Christian expressions. Uneducated and unauthorized preachers shared the gospel in plain language. Women and slaves participated in at-home Bible studies. Even children who demonstrated spiritual sensitivity became exemplars of Christian piety and morality. Described in organizational terms, it was the beginning of the decentralization of religious authority in America. Described in more politicized terms, it was the beginning of the democratization of American Christianity. The immediate consequence of this shift in New England was division among the churches.

The first phase of division was fallout along the lines of those who supported the Awakening and those who didn't. Supporters of the Awakening—men like Backus—became known as "New Lights." Those who opposed it were called "Old Lights." Charles Chauncy was a proud Old Light. In a scathing treatise called *Seasonable Thoughts on the State of Religion in New England*, Chauncy claimed that the radicals who were set ablaze during the Awakening were just the latest wave of "enthusiasts" in New England bent on destroying civilization as we knew it. These New Lights were the most recent iteration of those "who, through an excess of heat in their imaginations, had been betrayed into various unsound and dangerous opinions."

Chauncy found more than three hundred pages worth of charges to bring against the New Lights. Among the "bad and dangerous" developments for which New Lights were responsible, Chauncy decried itinerant preaching, the practice of preachers delivering sermons from town to town. He critiqued the emotional excesses of the movement, including "groaning, crying out, falling down and screaming." Most interesting (to me) is what Chauncy considered the movement's chief problem: "a presumptuous dependence on the blessed Spirit."

Chauncy believed, as most Christians surely did at the time, that believers should depend on the Holy Spirit. But the New Lights *presumed* upon the Spirit in a number of ways. They "despised" human learning, often preaching against New England's seminaries. The seminaries, Chauncy argued, were a gift from God. Rejecting them to demand a direct word from God *presumed* upon the Holy Spirit. Rejecting God's good gift and demanding a different one was audacious at best and ungrateful at worst. Chauncy believed that New Lights were so eager to hear a *new* word from God that they neglected God's word in the Scriptures. The revivalists wanted their revelation fresh and direct, Chauncy charged, and this made them and their interpretations accountable to no one. In short, some who wore the title Old Light did so proudly, as they considered themselves the protectors of true faith in New England.

As tensions grew between those who supported the Awakening and those who opposed it, the relationships between a number of pastors and their congregations became strained. For a season, many New Lights remained in their churches and held out hope that the Holy Spirit eventually would revive the entire congregation. As time passed, though, many lost hope this would happen. Some believed the vast majority of congregants were unconverted, nominal Christians. Some continued to believe their ministers, too, were unconverted. So the second phase of division inspired by the Awakening came when some New Lights became convinced that it was impossible to reform their current churches. It was time to leave them and start new ones. These New Lights who withdrew from their churches became known as "Separates." A favorite Scripture among them was 2 Corinthians 6:17—"Come out from among them, and be ye separate."

Isaac Backus participated in both of these stages of division. When Backus experienced conversion in 1741, he became a

New Light. Despite his discomfort with the Half-Way Covenant and his pastor's disapproval of the Awakening, he ultimately joined the local Congregational church in his hometown of Norwich, Connecticut. Since the founding of Boston in 1630, one key requirement of church membership had been that the candidate for membership had to give an account of his or her conversion experience—their personal testimony of saving faith. The Half-Way Covenant eliminated this requirement. Halfway membership meant that the children of full members who upheld Christian morals could be baptized in the church and partake in the Lord's Supper. The only thing they couldn't do—the last privilege reserved for full membership—was vote in church business.

The ministers who supported halfway membership did so for noble pastoral reasons. Maybe by partaking in the Lord's Supper, they thought, these halfway members would encounter the Holy Spirit and experience true personal conversion. Better to keep them in communion with God's people in Christian worship until that time came than to exclude them from worship and hope they have a converting experience somewhere else. Even so, New Lights viewed this accommodation as too great a compromise.

Backus tried to give his church the benefit of the doubt. But ultimately he could not reconcile himself to the practice of treating people like Christians who had not made a profession of faith. He thought halfway membership gave people false confidence in their salvation. After all, they were enjoying all the benefits of full membership (except for voting on church business). What motivation would they have to search their souls and someday make a full confession of faith?

What was worse, in Backus's view, is what the Half-Way Covenant represented. The measure was evidence in Backus's mind that New England's spiritual leaders no longer understood what the true church really was. If a personal testimony is required for church membership, that implies the church is made up only of authentic, born-again believers. Increasingly, though, New Englanders viewed church as the home of both converted and unconverted people. It was the home of the wheat and the tares (Mt 13:24-30). No sense trying to separate them now. God will do that at the final judgment. The revival preaching of the Awakening confronted sinners with their wretchedness and forced a moment of decision. Halfway membership provided a path of baby steps that may or may not result in saving faith. This turned the true spiritual church into a social gathering. How could a true believer be part of such a gathering?

Backus wrestled with these questions for ten months before finally, reluctantly, he joined the church, hoping he and other born-again members could reform its membership practice. They didn't. "I had now and then some refreshments," Backus wrote of his time in the Norwich Congregational Church, "but generally was cold and dull." Near the end of 1744, Backus realized there was no future for him there. "The Lord brought me to see," he wrote in his journal, "that though they had a form of godliness yet they did deny the power thereof and therefore I was commanded to turn away from them." Before the close of 1744—just three years after his salvation experience and after only two years of church membership—Backus and his mother, along with several of the most prominent families in town, left the Norwich standing church and began holding their own worship meetings. They became Separates.

Separate Worship and the Gifts of the Spirit

In twenty-first-century America, if you decide to leave your church, there is likely another one across the street that will be happy to have you. The menu of religious offerings was much shorter in Backus's eighteenth-century New England.

The most pressing practical question for Separates like Backus was where they should go to worship. Besides Congregational congregations, there were Baptist and Quaker fellowships. But Backus wasn't changing denominational affiliation. Beyond his understanding of what makes a church a *true* church, his beliefs hardly changed at all. Doctrinally he was a Calvinist, as he had always been. He still believed that infants with converted parents should be baptized as a sign of God's covenant. That meant he wasn't Baptist. He certainly wasn't Quaker.

The only theological convictions that divided Backus and his friends from their home church was that they believed the church should be a fellowship of believers *only* (not a mixed fellowship of converted and unconverted people), and therefore members must give a public testimony of their conversion experience. Neither of these convictions was new. They were commitments the Congregational Church once held (and indeed some Congregationalists continued to hold in the eighteenth century). As far as Backus was concerned, he wasn't establishing a new form of church. He was recovering an old form.

Because there was nowhere else for them to go, the handful of faithful folks who left the Norwich church with Backus met together in one another's homes "from time to time" for the next couple of years. On July 16, 1746, Backus and nine others joined in covenant to become a Separate church. They continued to meet in homes, but now their gatherings had a more formal title. They were a congregation of saints, truly converted, called the Bean Hill Separate Church.

Laborer for the Harvest

Backus was a farmer at this point in his story, and a successful one at that. But one morning he began to feel stirrings that he interpreted as the voice of the Holy Spirit. He began to wonder if God might have a new vocation in mind for him. A fellow believer was reading from Matthew 9:38 at a worship service: "Pray ye therefore the Lord of the harvest, that he will send forth labourers into his harvest." It was at that moment Backus realized "that the gifts that he had given me, did belong to the church and that while I neglected to improve [i.e., exercise] them—I robbed the church of their right."

Backus was untrained and averse to the spotlight. Thus he was resistant to the idea at first, but he continued to wrestle with it. On the morning of September 27, when Backus woke, "the hand of the Lord was powerfully upon me; and that day he gave me some clear views, of the state of his people, and also renewedly opened the treasures of the gospel; and commanded me to go and feed his people in his name."

God's call was clear to Backus, but he had his objections. To begin with, what God was asking him to do was illegal. He and his fellow Separates were already holding unauthorized meetings, which opened them to the consequence of fines. Becoming the visible leader of a group of Separates made him a target for the authorities. To be a pastor in Congregationalist New England, a candidate had to be approved by the other local Congregational ministers. Backus had no such approval. To be approved, a candidate had to be educated in an approved university. Backus had no such education. Preaching without an education and without approval would make him an "unlicensed preacher." Connecticut imprisoned many unlicensed preachers in the 1740s. Backus's status as a member of a founding family of the town, a wealthy farmer, and man of integrity couldn't protect him from fines, arrest, and imprisonment for preaching without permission. The liberty many Americans take for granted centuries after Backus was costly in the eighteenth century. Before he surrendered to God's calling, he took time to count the cost.

Perhaps it was the libertarian zeal Backus inherited that steeled his nerves. Backus himself gives credit to the Holy Spirit. In relatively short order, God "spoke them words with power to my soul: my grace shall be sufficient for thee." He preached his first sermon that same week to the Bean Hill Separate congregation—a reflection on Psalm 53. It's impossible to know for sure how Backus interpreted and applied that psalm for his contemporaries. Backus rarely wrote down his sermons after preaching them and rarely outlined them beforehand. But a little conjecture is possible. Here's the text of Psalm 53:

> The fool hath said in his heart, There is no God. Corrupt are they, and have done abominable iniquity: there is none that doeth good.
>
> God looked down from heaven upon the children of men, to see if there were any that did understand, that did seek God.
>
> Every one of them is gone back: they are altogether become filthy; there is none that doeth good, no, not one.
>
> Have the workers of iniquity no knowledge? who eat up my people as they eat bread: they have not called upon God.
>
> There were they in great fear, where no fear was: for God hath scattered the bones of him that encampeth against thee: thou hast put them to shame, because God hath despised them.
>
> Oh that the salvation of Israel were come out of Zion! When God bringeth back the captivity of his people, Jacob shall rejoice, and Israel shall be glad.

It's likely Backus saw his own generation reflected in Psalm 53:2-3. Even then in the 1740s, God was looking down on his people to see "if there were any that did understand, that did seek God." Unfortunately, the clear answer from Backus's point of view was no: "there is none that doeth good, no, not one." His generation was in a state of decline. But the Awakening inaugurated a change. God was bringing his people back from captivity. "Jacob shall rejoice, and Israel shall be glad."

Evidently, Backus's first sermon was good enough to convince his fellow Separates in Bean Hill that God had gifted him to preach the gospel. By 1746, then, Backus was a preacher, but not yet a pastor. He spent the next couple of years itinerating around the region, preaching in the homes of Separate brethren around New England and seeing evidence, again and again, of God's renewing and converting work. A journal entry from 1747 illustrates what those meetings looked like:

> Though it was extraordinary bad traveling and very cold yet there came a great number of people together, and Brother Snow preached in the forenoon . . . and he had clearness and assistance therein: and when he had done I stood up and began to exhort and Divine truth seemed to flow through my soul like a river; and after I had spoken for some time I stopped and only turning round to look on some others, Truth would flow in again; so that it seemed easier to speak than to let it alone: and *thus I went on for several hours*, and saints were wonderfully refreshed and many sinners struck under conviction. And towards night I preached from the 2nd Psalm, and had as great or greater assistance and freedom than I ever before had in my life and there was a great moving on the minds of the people: glory to God alone.

Backus's account of the day's preaching—not just the *morning*!—reveals a theme that developed in his writing and that ultimately gave him the courage to preach, despite his lack of formal education and the imminent legal consequences of preaching without authorization. Backus put his confidence not in study or formal preparation but in "assistance and freedom" from the Holy Spirit at the moment of preaching. He considered himself a conduit for God's words.

Often that meant God's word flowed through him with ease. Other times there was a blockage in the conduit and the preaching didn't go so well.

On February 18, 1748, a Thursday night, Backus preached at a home where instead of being free and assisted, he was "very much shut up." For this, Backus wrote, "I desire to be humbled by God." It is worth pointing out that the Great Awakening inspired the kind of preaching that brought it about. Free, emotional, extemporaneous, and plain-spoken sermons were rare before the Awakening, before people like Whitefield proved what they could accomplish in the right hands. After the Awakening, this style of preaching became common for New Lights.

In any case, it was a critical New Light conviction that it was not a committee's decision and a good education that made a man a pastor, but an internal call from God and the gifts of the Holy Spirit. From there, it was not up to a council to decide. All authority for confirming the gifts and calling a pastor resided in the local congregation. Backus believed the Spirit and the church had spoken, and that was that.

Hungering After Gospel Food

In addition to giving Backus an opportunity to improve his gift to preach and clarify his calling, itinerating introduced Backus to two of the most important relationships of his life. While traveling to preach, Backus first visited Titicut parish, some ninety miles west of his home in Norwich. The good people of Titicut eventually became the first congregation Backus served as a pastor.

On December 19, 1747, Backus had a vision of his future ministry in Titicut. For several days, Backus traveled the town speaking with the locals and felt blessed that spiritual conversation came easily with them. He recorded in his journal that they "appeared to be really hungering after gospel food." One evening as Backus shared dinner with some members of the community, he sensed God speak to him again through a familiar passage. "As we were setting down to eat," Backus wrote, "'em words in John 4:35 to 38, were brought in with great clearness and power upon my soul":

> Say not ye, There are yet four months, and then cometh harvest? behold, I say unto you, Lift up your eyes, and look on the fields; for they are white already to harvest.
>
> And he that reapeth receiveth wages, and gathereth fruit unto life eternal: that both he that soweth and he that reapeth may rejoice together.
>
> And herein is that saying true, One soweth, and another reapeth.

> I sent you to reap that whereon ye bestowed no labour: other men laboured, and ye are entered into their labours.

There at the dinner table, "I was led to view a large field all white to harvest here." Other pastors had been active in the area, both during the Awakening and after. They had accomplished a lot. But now Backus's

> soul was constrained by divine light, love, and power to enter into their labours; and my heart was so drawn forth towards God, and in love to his people here that I felt willing to impart not only the Gospel to them but my own soul also, because they were made dear unto me; though I knew none of them personally.

On that day, over that meal, "these cords of truth and love that bound my soul now to this people, I never could get off by any means."

Backus spent enough time in the Titicut parish that local officials approached him and asked him to become the local pastor. The fact that they offered him the position shows how deeply the Awakening had shaped that particular part of the colony. Trouble was, by human standards, he was unqualified. He didn't have the requisite education. Titicut's officials were willing to overlook that fact, but they were not prepared to waive the second requirement. To take the post, Backus would have to be "examined and come in regularly," which meant being approved by a council of ministers in the region.

Instead of viewing the offer as an opportunity, Backus saw it as a trap. He interpreted it as a snare designed by the devil to catch him and keep him from doing what he was called to do. He was so committed to his belief that it was an internal call and a congregation's affirmation that settled the relationship of pastor and parish that he refused to cooperate with Titicut's leadership. He told the authorities they were welcome to hear him preach, if they wanted to. And "I told 'em if they were a mind to get any neighbouring ministers to come and examine me I was free to preach to 'em or to give 'em the reasons of my hope or of my practice." But he didn't grant them authority to affirm or deny his call. "I shouldn't leave it to man whether I should preach the Gospel or no." It might have been expedient for Backus to receive the formal endorsement of established ministers in the area. They may have approved him despite his lack of formal education, because settling a Separate minister might have brought some peace to the region. But Backus stood on principle. It wouldn't be the last time.

A Suitable Helper

The other important relationship that got its start in these early years of Backus's traveling ministry was between him and Susanna Mason of Rehoboth, Massachusetts. Frequent visits to Rehoboth during his preaching journeys put Backus and Susanna in regular contact between 1746 and 1748. By the summer of 1748, Backus "thought it to be my duty to seek for an agreeable companion," someone to share life and ministry with. Those sentiments are not exactly romantic by modern standards, but they got him praying for a wife.

As in all things, Backus wanted to go about this decision the right way. He dedicated the full day on August 15 to fasting and prayer, specifically requesting that God would shed light on his search for a mate. It was during that day of fasting and prayer Backus felt God impress on his heart that he had chosen Susanna to be his wife.

It took a while for him to follow through, but in January 1749 Backus traveled to visit Susanna to discuss the prospect of marriage with her. He visited her again in March, at which point he recorded after the fact, "our minds appeared to harmonize in the design" to marry. Again, this sounds more rational than romantic. But once they set their mind to marriage, they moved quickly. They were engaged in September and married in November. Ever the pastor, Backus officiated his own wedding. After a brief reading from Scripture and after the congregation sang a couple of psalms, Backus preached a short sermon.

He rarely wrote about Susanna or their children in his diary. His diary was almost exclusively a record of his ministry and travels. We have no record of Susanna's feelings about her husband. But there's ample evidence that the seemingly unromantic diary entries related to their courtship tell only part of the story. Later in life Backus said about his wedding, "I think I can truly say that Jesus and his disciples were at the wedding. My soul is astonished at the goodness of God. Oh, that I may never forget His benefits!" Looking back at his life in his eighties,

Backus called Susanna "the greatest temporal blessing which God ever gave me; for which I trust I shall praise him to eternity." Isaac and Susanna were married almost fifty-one years and raised nine children together.

Between February 12 and 16, Backus met with sixteen Christian men and women who shared testimonies of their conversions and "what the Lord had done for their souls." In a midweek assembly at someone's home, the group signed the articles of formation and covenant for membership and officially formed "The Church of Christ in the Joining Borders of Bridgewater & Middleborough" (i.e., Titicut parish), and Backus was ordained as its pastor. Called, married, and hired to pastor his first church—Isaac was twenty-four years old.

Not only did the Church of Christ in the Joining Borders of Bridgewater & Middleborough have the distinction of having an exceedingly long name, it was also a dynamic, growing congregation. Backus preached nearly every night of the week. The church began with sixteen members. By March, they were up to thirty. But they remained a congregation without a building, so they continued to meet in peoples' homes. One week in March, Backus preached in the homes of nine different church members. The congregation practiced what it preached with regard to church membership. Backus records that he met in the home of "Brother Phinney" on a Tuesday night, on which night Brother Phinney and his wife joined the church. Not everyone made the cut, though. One woman present that night was offended because she was not accepted into membership.

The church faced other challenges in addition to a lack of property. As the congregation in Titicut grew, Backus experienced increasing opposition from Old Lights and others who objected to the unlawful worship he and his congregation were conducting. Opposition came initially in the form of slander. Rumor spread that Backus had multiple wives in a handful of country hamlets, and that he had bastard children scattered across Connecticut. The citizens of one town were so convinced that Backus had illegitimate children in that very town that they denied him entry and banned him for good. Rather than discourage him, the opposition confirmed for Backus that he was doing God's work in a hostile world. After all, Jesus had said, "In the world ye shall have tribulation."

He also said, "Be of good cheer; I have overcome the world" (Jn 16:33).

Managing Marginalization

Twenty-first-century evangelicalism shares a lot with the New Lights and Separates who emerged from the Great Awakening. Different denominations and traditions reflect this value differently, but most evangelicals agree that conversion is a crucial element of true faith. A person cannot be *born* a Christian; they become a Christian by being *re*born. Thus the term *born-again Christian*, an important identifier in American faith and politics, is an inheritance of the Awakening. Both the need for a personal experience of salvation and the personal testimony itself so prevalent in many evangelical circles are specific examples of how the Awakening era has influenced our Christian practice today. Whether we know the history or not, the instincts and identities of modern evangelicals is profoundly shaped by the experiences of men and women from Backus's generation.

Another remnant of evangelical America's Awakening heritage is a sense of embattlement in the American Christian psyche. Beginning in the mid-1700s, evangelicals like Backus began to view themselves as the remnant few "true believers" standing firm against a hostile and unbelieving world in which traditional values were constantly under attack. Even though they were a new group, they viewed themselves as recovering commitments that had been lost. In this way they were trying to preserve a traditional value that had been tossed aside by their opponents. Many Christians on this side of the Awakening may be tempted to agree with them, as evangelicals tend to view the Awakening as the work of God in history. Those who opposed it must have been opposing God himself. It's important to remember, though, that Old Lights like Chauncy sincerely believed *they* were the ones protecting and preserving the work of God in America. *They* increasingly imagined *themselves* as the shrinking army of faithful believers. The sense of marginalization applied in both directions.

I can't prove causation between these things, but it seems American Christians have never shaken this deep sense of marginalization and embattlement. In fact it seems all parties in American public life view themselves as the embattled minority.

White nationalists fighting to preserve Confederate monuments see themselves as the defenders of common sense at war with the mainstream, liberal media. Liberals in America view themselves as the lone voice of sanity in a nation of racists and misogynists. Progressives feel hamstrung by the power of the religious right. Conservatives feel suppressed by liberal Hollywood and a godless national government. What these groups have in common is the shared belief that they are the underdog and the last best hope for civilization. This is a very poor starting point for dialogue.

There's more to say about his later. The important point to note now is that there is a difference between *being* marginalized and *feeling* marginalized.

Historically speaking, Backus was right about his status as a marginalized member of society. Fortunately, he managed to fight for freedom without playing the victim. He managed to articulate visions of both the past and the future that his generation found compelling enough to embrace. He managed to move his embattled group from the margins to the center of American public life.

But before things got better, they got worse.

THREE

BECOMING BAPTIST

No man who has not experienced the like can form a proper idea of the distress I endured for two years.

Isaac Backus, *Diary of Isaac Backus*

There was very little upside to becoming a Baptist in New England before 1728.

Before—and even after—that date, Baptists were a marginalized and frequently persecuted minority in New England. In 1645, just fifteen years after the settlers of Massachusetts Bay founded the colony as a place to experiment with religious liberty, the General Court passed a law that banned Baptists from the colony altogether. In the minds of Massachusetts' authorities, the Baptists erred in at least two ways. First, they refused to baptize their infants, and this was considered both a spiritual error and a threat to the public good. Second, many New England Baptists were, in the seventeenth century, Arminian in theology. They rejected the Calvinist doctrines of limited atonement and predestination. They were, in short, entirely unacceptable.

Today many evangelicals who disagree about baptism and the finer points of doctrine nevertheless accept one another as brothers and sisters in Christ. This was not the case in colonial New England. It was the Baptists' commitment to believer's baptism in particular that set them apart for special disdain. Public sentiments about Baptists at the time are clearly articulated in the court's statement:

> Forasmuch as experience has plentifully and often proven that since the first rising of the Anabaptists about a hundred years since they have been the incendiaries of the commonwealths and the infectors of persons in main matters of religion and troublers of churches in all places where they have been.

As *incendiaries*, *infectors*, and *troublers,* the Baptists were unwelcome in Massachusetts Bay Colony for a time. Banishment moreover was not simple spiritual excommunication. It was enforced by the political arm of the local government. Any Baptist who returned to the colony was subject to consequences in the form of fines, imprisonment, and corporal punishment.

Where Baptists *were* allowed to reside, they were required to pay a poll tax every election season, and the revenue from those taxes helped pay the salary of the local established pastor and fund repairs to the local church building. Every citizen was required to pay the religious tax, not just Baptists. But for Baptists it was a special burden, considering they didn't attend the church led by the pastor the taxes supported. Instead, they paid the tax and attended church elsewhere, where they *also* paid the salary of their own pastor through voluntary tithes and offerings.

Tax Relief and Its Complications

Baptists received some relief in 1728, when English authorities demanded that New England legislators exempt Baptists from religious taxes. Baptists weren't the only group that benefited. The law applied, under a couple of conditions, to both Baptists and Quakers, who claimed to oppose the tax on grounds of conscience. The law required that anyone released from the poll tax must attend worship regularly somewhere and live within five miles of the church they attended.

The legislation was a Pyrrhic victory. It relieved the financial burden of taxation, but it increased the resentment of the Baptist's non-Baptist neighbors. A town with a large population of tax-exempt citizens suddenly lost considerable tax revenue to pay its clergy. That meant the remaining taxpayers had to pay more per person, now that Baptists and Quakers were excluded. As you might imagine, this change did not receive strong popular support. If the Standing Order members questioned the Baptists' doctrine before, now they questioned the Baptists' motives. It was common for those who were baptized as adults and joined a Baptist church to be greeted sarcastically by their neighbors from then on: "Ah, Mr. neighbor Smith, I hear you have been dipped [i.e., baptized] to wash away your taxes."

So the legislation of 1728 theoretically freed Baptists and Quakers from the burden of religious taxes. Unfortunately, the new law didn't necessarily change how individual tax assessors conducted business. Some assessors continued to demand that Baptists and Quakers pay their religious taxes unless they could *prove* their religious affiliations. That was the rub—how might a person *prove* they regularly attended a church five miles away that no one else in town attended? And how could they *prove* they were sincere in their religious beliefs and not simply dodging taxes? The closest modern analogue I can think of has to do with Christians and same-sex marriage. How would you *prove* that you oppose same-sex marriage on theological grounds, and not simply because you're homophobic?

Before there were apps to solve all problems, there were legal ordinances. A new law in 1734 was designed to eliminate the guesswork in determining who was required to pay taxes and who was exempt. The law eventually required that the town clerk maintain two lists—one a registry of Baptists and the other a registry of Quakers. If someone's name was on one of those lists, he or she was exempt from religious tax. Every year before tax season rolled around, citizens were invited to review the list. If someone's name was not on the list, they could have it added. To do so they were required to bring two witnesses with them, two members of the church they claimed to attend, to vouch that they were in fact members in good standing. In theory, this was easy enough.

These laws exempting Baptists (and Quakers) from religious taxes were passed before the Great Awakening, when the percentage of dissenters in most New England towns was relatively small. As we have seen, the balance began to shift after the Awakening. Suddenly, large numbers of people who claimed to experience new birth during the Awakening were leaving their established churches (churches supported by taxation) to form Separate churches. This introduced a new challenge for the courts. The Separate churches now forming were not Baptist or Quaker. Doctrinally and theologically, many of the Separates affirmed all the same creeds and confessions as the churches they left. The only difference between them was that they simply emphasized the importance of spiritual new birth and the holiness of the local church. They did not constitute a recognized sect or denomination. For this reason—because they were not Baptists or Quakers—they were not exempt from religious taxation.

Eventually some Separates' doctrinal commitments evolved. Some of them began breaking away from the Separate churches and becoming Baptists. Isaac Backus found himself in exactly this situation in the late 1740s and early 1750s.

Gradually and Reluctantly Baptist

The transition from Separate to Baptist was not altogether dramatic. It wasn't like a Pentecostal adopting Judaism or a Catholic becoming Buddhist. That is, it didn't necessarily require a drastic change in belief. Many Separate churches shared a lot in common theologically with the older Baptist churches that had been around—and more or less outlawed—for a century or more. Separates agreed with Baptists about church membership: only those who were regenerated and gave a convincing testimony of their conversion could join the congregation. Like the Separates, Baptists rejected halfway membership. Additionally, Separates agreed with Baptists that a pastor should be chosen by the local congregation and not appointed by a council of ministers. Many Separates agreed with Baptists, furthermore, that pastors should be paid by the voluntary offering of their parishioners and not by a tax of the general population. They agreed on nearly everything, in fact, except for baptism. On this point they disagreed, as they put it, about who was "qualified" for baptism: were infants, the children of born-again believers, appropriate candidates? Or was it only adult believers who could be immersed?

When Backus formed the church in Titicut parish, he formed it as a Separate church that retained the practice of infant baptism. He had some misgivings about baptism because he couldn't settle in his mind how the ordinance was related to church membership. He viewed the church as a fellowship of born-again Christians. Infants who have been baptized have not been born again. So, from time to time, he was struck by the question, "Where, and in what relation to the church of God do those stand who have been baptized and yet are not believers?"

This was *the* central question for a man in his situation. With a profound sense of conviction, he left a church that practiced halfway membership because he believed the practice undermined the value of personal regeneration. He believed halfway membership violated the true nature of the church as a gathering of born-again members only. And yet he maintained the practice at the heart of halfway membership: infant baptism.

Some churches handled the apparent inconsistency by choosing to agree to disagree. Some, for example, acknowledged in their founding articles that while the majority of congregants recognized the validity of infant baptism, some did not. Some had their newborn babies baptized; others abstained. Differing opinions on that one matter generally were not regarded as reason enough to break fellowship, considering the people agreed on all other matters. Many Separate churches maintained the tension of disagreement on the issue of baptism for as long as they could. For his part, Backus simply avoided the question until he couldn't any longer. The year was 1749.

For a host of reasons, 1749 was a difficult year for Backus and the Titicut congregation. As in the years before the Awakening, young people began to show signs of spiritual apathy. Whispering and backbiting became a problem among the youth. Older adults had their own problems. They lost interest in the lengthy preaching meetings that characterized their early gatherings. They lost enthusiasm in worship, lost their sense of urgency about the gospel and its demands. Some of the sins that Backus's parishioners were committing sound harmless today. He lamented that the big issues were "particularly fine dressing—and speaking against and despising one another."

Beyond particular sins, though, there was a general sense of spiritual decline. Backus uses the terms *dull*, *cold*, and *hard* time and again in his journals to describe his church's spiritual climate in this season. There were moments of relief, when Backus felt freedom in his preaching and his congregation appeared receptive to the work of the Holy Spirit. But an overwhelming melancholy rested on the congregation through most of the year. Backus sensed it in his people. He felt it in himself. "I have been under great trials, the bigger part of this month passed," he wrote in April, "often born down with discouragements, and the people in general have been very cold and dull."

The new year did not bring relief; 1750 was just as bad. On New Year's Eve 1750, Backus wrote, "Alas! I had but a poor ending of the year. This year 1750 throughout almost the whole of it has been a season of heavy trial on my soul."

While Backus and members of his congregation had discussed the question of baptism in the past, during this season of general spiritual decline they started earnestly debating the practice. Before now, they had agreed to disagree. Now they openly debated who should be baptized and how.

When the debates began, Backus, who affirmed infant baptism himself, wondered if there may be some mischief in the very idea of believer's baptism. Maybe the reason his people were so ornery all of the sudden is because they were entertaining this Baptist notion. Gradually, though, he began to see the issue from both sides. For two years, between 1749 and 1751, he vacillated. He was at turns equally convinced of both views of the ordinance. Sometimes he changed his position within a matter of days.

One Saturday in August 1749, for example, he dedicated a day to study, fasting, and prayer, in which he asked God for clear insight about baptism. He wanted to end the day decided, once and for all. God answered, Backus thought. The next morning he was so confident that he preached from Romans 6:4: "Therefore we are buried with him by baptism into death: that like as Christ was raised up from the dead by the glory of the Father, even so we also should walk in newness of life." Using this passage as his foundation, Backus argued only adult believers can experience this transformation from death to life, upon their personal confession of faith. And they should testify to their faith by being immersed in water (or "plunging" as he called it), not sprinkling. Being plunged is a symbol of burial, and coming out of the water is a symbol of resurrection. The apostle Paul was clear. The matter was settled.

Except that it wasn't. By the end of the day Backus regretted preaching on the subject. By Tuesday he was an avowed proponent of infant baptism again.

While Backus inched his way toward a decision, certain members of his congregation took a more direct approach. Backus left town for a stint of itinerant preaching. He did this periodically to encourage fellow pastors in the region, and this particular trip kept him away from Titicut for nearly a month. If he was hoping the time would provide a season of refreshment, he was surely disappointed. Rumors greeted him on the road that there had been something of a coup in his church while he was away. When he returned home he discovered that while he was gone some members of his congregation invited a Baptist pastor from another town to come baptize them. Nine adults from Backus's church were plunged in his absence.

Backus addressed the situation from the pulpit the next Sunday. He preached on baptism again and spoke passionately and with great conviction this time in *favor* of baptizing infants. He had been wrong before, he admitted. Infants *should* be baptized. The nine people who had been plunged were offended by the sermon and they met together in their own worship service the following Sunday. The irony of this move is palpable. Members of Backus's Separate congregation were now separated and holding their own services.

Instead of mending fences, Backus dug in his heels. He declared that he was "willing to venture into eternity" affirming infant baptism. This statement, too, proved to be rash. For the better part of the next two years, Backus wrestled with both a general melancholy and dissatisfaction with his congregation and a deep sense of inner turmoil about the nature of baptism. "No man," Backus exclaimed, "who has not experienced the like, can form a proper idea of the distress I endured for two years."

Exhausted by his own lack of certainty, he finally set aside July 20, 1751, "as a day of secret fasting and prayer, to seek once more the direction of God." He ended the day convinced the Baptists were right. This time his conviction stuck. Just over a month later, Backus was baptized along with six members of his church, upon their profession of faith in Jesus Christ.

This was ten years after his conversion.

Another New Beginning

The good news was that Backus's mind was now settled on the subject. The bad news was that his decision put him at odds with many of the members of his own church. As a pastor, Backus was deeply committed to the unity of his congregation and desired to continue to serve them—*all* of them—as their shepherd. Initially he proposed a compromise. Personally, he was Baptist, he explained. But the congregation needn't be. His conscience would not allow himself to baptize infants himself now that he was convinced the Bible opposed the practice. But, like other Separates before him, he didn't consider a disagreement over baptism a sufficient reason to break fellowship. The solution he suggested was cumbersome but conciliatory. He offered to invite clergymen from other churches or towns to baptize infants, as the need arose, for members of the church who were committed to that tradition. As for him, he would baptize the adults.

The arrangement sounds impractical and even implausible today, but the pastor's heart was in the right place. Surely, he thought, there's a way to maintain Christian fellowship—*not just in the abstract but within the covenant of a local church*—in a way that preserves each individual's right to liberty of conscience. Baptism was important. Of course it was. But it was essentially the only point of doctrine over which the congregation was divided. It may have been a desperate proposal. It was certainly a deeply sensitive proposal.

But it didn't work. The damage of two years of general spiritual decline and theological infighting had been done.

Backus stepped down from his duties as pastor for a brief period and traveled with his wife and mother in search, one assumes, of perspective. He was sure of two things. First, he was now a committed Baptist. Second, he still was called to preach the gospel. Over the course of several months, Backus and the Titicut parish and even a larger group of Separate New Light churches convened a host of council meetings to determine how to mediate disagreements like this one in the future. They were a fledgling movement still figuring out how to operate. Years of dialogue followed until finally, in January 1756, Backus and six members of his church "entered into covenant as a Baptist church" in nearby Middleboro. The six members who went with him voted unanimously to make Backus their pastor.

Conscience and Humility

Backus's waffling on baptism was somewhat uncharacteristic. Yes, his convictions about other theological and social issues deepened or evolved over time. His faith was far from static. But baptism is the only issue about which he sincerely struggled to find clear, consistent footing. This is the part of Backus's story that most attracted me to him when I first stumbled on him.

My spiritual journey took me roughly the same length of time Backus's took him—about a decade—although I made the journey in the opposite direction. Backus's spiritual sojourn led him to embrace Baptist doctrine. Mine led me away from Baptist doctrine and, ultimately, to embrace Presbyterianism. (My friend Isaac would be very disappointed.) In the decade or so after college, I wrestled with many of the same questions Backus wrestled with. What is the true nature of the church? What is the relationship between the church and the children of believers? When does someone pass from darkness to light, and how do you mark that transition? Does it happen in a moment or over a period of weeks and months and years? My answers to those questions are neither terribly interesting nor relevant to this discussion.

The significant point, I suppose, is that even though my journey and Backus's led in opposite directions and resulted in our taking up opposing points of view, I was profoundly comforted by the honesty and humility with which he made his journey.

One thing I craved during my years of questions was an open forum in which to discuss the doubts and confusions I was wrestling with. I found venues in higher education. But I really wanted to have the conversations within the local church. Ironically, I was part of a congregation that celebrated "soul liberty" and "liberty of conscience," but I never felt safe to ask questions there. My experiences combined with Backus's story have convinced me that our view of religious liberty has to be large enough to encompass those we disagree with. Surely this is the first step, long before we start marching and carrying signs in the streets. First comes developing a church culture in which warm and committed relationships create space for disagreeing with members of our own faith family. Maybe Backus and I are both naive, but I'm convinced it should be entirely possible for fellow believers to disagree about important theological and political and social issues without breaking fellowship.

One reason for this is because all of our convictions are developing. This doesn't mean that all of our convictions will change altogether. But some of them will. At some point in our lives we will all denounce with great gusto some opinion an earlier version of ourselves promoted with great gusto. Most of our convictions will not change altogether, but the intensity with which we hold them, or the priority they occupy in our minds, will increase or decrease over time. The fact that God is sovereign—or that he is gracious or that he is just—may be *an* important fact to you during one season of life and it may be *the* important fact in another.

Public discourse in twenty-first-century America increasingly forces people to take firm stands and draw clear lines in the sand over a wide range of issues. This sort of tribalism ignores that basic fact that all opinions are under construction. Joining a tribe aborts the process. In the current sociopolitical climate, churches would do well to model the kind of accommodation Backus was willing to attempt regarding the issue of baptism in his church. He was willing to create a space in which people were free to journey together, in fellowship, toward the final form of their conviction. Yes, his proposal to have different ministers perform different modes of baptism was unrealistic. But it's a proposal that acknowledged the thorniness of the issues. It demonstrated charity in disagreement. And it no doubt issued from Backus's own self-awareness that he himself existed somewhere along a continuum of conviction on the issue of baptism. His instinct was to create a fellowship in which sincere and humble disagreement could be part of a healthy community. It's a beautiful ambition.

A second reason we ought to extend this posture of generous disagreement to one another is that the gospel makes us humble. Or it should. "I once was blind but now I see" is no simple platitude. It's the declaration of fact that there was a time when I got some important things all wrong. It should prompt us to assume that we will again in the future get something important all wrong. The way this point is different from the first is this: we should be patient with our brother because he may be wrong and someday he may be right. That's point one. Point two is that we should be patient with our sister because *we* may be wrong and someday we may realize it.

Another Day, Another Battle

Backus's decision about baptism created a new opportunity for him. His *Separate* church had not been eligible for tax exemption. Technically his *Baptist* congregation now was. But securing tax exemption was not a simple matter.

New England's lawmakers balked at the sudden rise in Baptist numbers during and after the Awakening. They recognized that if they allowed everyone who claimed to be Baptist to dodge their taxes, it would soon be impossible to pay Congregational pastors and maintain church facilities. Once the Baptists were exempt, the remaining Old Lights would have to make up the difference by paying considerably more per capita. The burden was simply too great.

As a result, in 1753, three years before Backus planted his Baptist congregation in Middleboro, Massachusetts, magistrates amended the exemption law to make it harder for these new Baptists to benefit from exemption status. For these new Baptist to be covered under the new legislation, they had to receive endorsements from three "Old Baptist" churches: congregations that had been Baptist since *before* the Awakening. This was a shrewd move. Essentially the law required any new Baptist church to receive a certificate from three different Old Baptist churches attesting that "they esteem such church to be one of their denomination." The trouble was that many of the older Baptist churches were Arminian in theology, while those who became Baptist during the Awakening were predominately Calvinist. The Old Baptists and new Baptists disagreed about enough that it was virtually impossible for a new church to locate three Old Baptist congregations willing to endorse the new one as one of their own.

Other towns sharpened the point of this new legislation with their own local ordinances. In some places, in addition to securing certificates from three existing Baptist churches, new congregations were also required to build a meetinghouse before they could apply for tax exemption. Of course, the whole time they were pooling their resources to build a meetinghouse and pay their pastor, they were still liable for ecclesiastical taxes. The likelihood of fulfilling both criteria—the three certificates and the meetinghouse—was basically zero.

But that was not all. In some places, there was a third requirement. In addition to the certificates and a worship space, a new congregation was also required to have hired a minister who had been approved by an association of local ministers. If the first two criteria—the certificates and meetinghouse—were theoretically possible, this third criterion was not. It was highly unlikely that a council of Standing Order pastors would approve a man like Isaac Backus. One minimum requirement for ordination was a formal education, which Backus (and most Baptist pastors at the time) didn't have.

So while Backus had settled the question of conscience regarding baptism, he wasn't finished. He increasingly recognized that the practice of infant baptism was closely connected to another critical issue: the relationship between church and state. Already he had dabbled in efforts to be released from the duty of religious taxes. But now that the issue of baptism was settled for him, the next major obstacle he faced was a civil government that retained the right to fine and even arrest him if he failed to pay another pastor's salary. He had only just begun fighting.

FOUR

NO MORE "NURSING FATHERS"

It is not the pence but the power that alarms us.

Isaac Backus, quoted in *A Memoir of the Life and Times of the Rev. Isaac Backus*

Article 1, section 7 of the Missouri Constitution prohibits the state from providing financial assistance directly to a church. This legislation created problems for Trinity Lutheran Church Child Learning Center, a preschool and daycare, which applied for one of the state's reimbursement grants after replacing the pea gravel on its playground with a pour-in-place rubber surface. "Although the Center ranked fifth out of the 44 applicants, it did not receive a grant because it is a church." Trinity Lutheran believed the state's actions violated the First Amendment of the US Constitution. The Federal District Court disagreed. It ruled that the Free Exercise Clause prohibits the government from *restricting* religious practice, "but it generally does not prohibit withholding an affirmative benefit on account of religion."

The case eventually made it to the Supreme Court, which ruled in 2016 that "the Department's policy violated the rights of Trinity Lutheran under the Free Exercise Clause of the First Amendment by denying the Church an otherwise available public benefit on account of its religious status."

If it is difficult for contemporary Americans to imagine an America in which the civil government has a right to impose taxes on its citizens to support the ministry of a particular church, it's because a certain understanding of church and state is enshrined in our founding documents. We may still be sorting out how to apply this understanding of church and state, as the case of Trinity Lutheran illustrates, but there is general agreement that the First Amendment to the US Constitution ensures the federal government will not privilege one religious group over another or limit any religious group's right to worship according to its conscience:

> Congress shall make no law respecting an establishment of religion, or prohibiting the free exercise thereof; or abridging the freedom of speech, or of the press; or the right of the people peaceably to assemble, and to petition the Government for a redress of grievances.

While this statement about the limit of government is fundamental to our understanding of religious life in America, a different arrangement dominated America, and New England especially, for more than a century before the Constitution. The First Amendment was adopted in 1791. That was fifteen years *after* the colonies declared independence from England. It was a full *half century* after Isaac Backus experienced new birth in the Great Awakening. For that long fifty years, religious minorities in New England struggled to climb out from under the burden of religious taxation.

The battle against ecclesiastical taxes was uphill for a number of reasons. One reason was, of course, that the Standing Order churches had a lot to lose if large numbers of citizens stopped paying the taxes. But there was another more fundamental challenge. Just as it is difficult for us to imagine a different relationship between church and state in America because our values are enshrined in our founding documents, the ruling powers of Backus's generation struggled to imagine a different relationship between church and state because *their* arrangement had been enshrined in *their* founding documents. It was part of their theological inheritance as Protestants. It was part of their social identity as the descendants of New England Puritans. Really and truly, it was presumptuous for dissenters like Backus to believe the Standing Order would agree without issue to dispensing with such an integral part of New England faith and practice.

By demanding tax exemption the dissenters were not merely asking for a change in policy. Dissenters like Isaac Backus and his Baptist congregation were asking, ultimately, to upend a centuries-old understanding of the roles of the church and civil government and how they related to each other. What's more, Congregationalists didn't just have history on their side. They believed they had the Bible on their side. By the early 1750s, the struggle for religious liberty became a battle for the Bible.

In Defense of "Nursing Fathers"

The Separates who left Standing Order churches after the Great Awakening claimed to do so because the churches they attended failed to uphold biblical standards for conversion and church membership. The Bible, and how it should be interpreted, became a critical element in the debate about the Awakening itself. So did issues that developed because of the Awakening, including religious taxation.

The battle over religious taxation took place very much in the public eye. Some ministers felt the need to remind the populace of the longstanding tradition of and biblical mandate for the tax before the Separates won everyone over to their way of thinking. Ministers published articles, printed pamphlets, and preached sermons with the goal of convincing dissenters—and reminding everyone else—of their duty to support the established pastor in town. An Election Day sermon from 1765, preached by Edward Dorr, pastor of the First Church in Hartford, Connecticut, lays out the biblical argument for the practice of religious taxation as the majority of New Englanders understood it at the time.

His text was one sentence from Isaiah 49. The context of Isaiah 49 is God's promise to restore Israel after the exile. It describes how Israel will prosper in the time of the Lord's favor, in the "day of salvation" (Is 49:8). The prophet promises that God will return his people to their land when the time of exile is complete (vv. 8-9). He will meet their material needs, filling them with good food and clean water (vv. 9-10). When God restores his people, the pagan nations will serve Israel (v. 22). This brings us to Dorr's text. The evidence that all God's promises have been fulfilled is found in Isaiah 49:23—"And kings shall be thy nursing fathers; and their queens thy nursing mothers." Dorr interpreted this passage not simply as a promise but as a command. "This much may fairly be inferred from the text," Dorr argued, "that civil rulers *ought to be* nursing fathers to the church." And what does a "nursing father" do, exactly? Well, because religion cannot "be supported and maintained in the world, without some expense," the civil government is obliged to promote religion through taxation.

Leaving aside for a moment that the image of a "nursing father" is a strange one, this interpretation of Isaiah 49:23 illustrates just how different the mental framework was for discussions about religious liberty in the eighteenth century. Present-day interpreters of Isaiah 49 do not assume that the Bible is here commanding religious taxation. Our assumption that church and state should be separate and independent makes that interpretation impossible. For Dorr, by contrast, who assumed that the state should support the church, this was the only possible interpretation of the text available to him.

Pastor Dorr interpreted Isaiah 49:23 the way most Christians had for at least two centuries. In Protestantism, the church-state application of Isaiah 49:23 dates back to John Calvin, and his interpretation was already characteristic of Roman Catholicism before him. Calvin, whose Reformed theological system dominated Puritan New England, offered a nuanced interpretation of Isaiah 49:23. He believed, first, that it was a prophecy that has already been fulfilled. It refers to a time when formerly hostile forces acknowledge Christ as true God and worship him appropriately. This happened, Calvin claimed, when emperors like Constantine "not only submitted to the yoke of Christ, but likewise contributed their riches to raise up and maintain the Church of Christ, so as to be her guardians and defenders." So Isaiah 49:23 *has been* fulfilled. However, it also must be fulfilled again in the future. In addition to reading the verse as fulfilled promise, Calvin also read the clause "kings shall be" as a present command for magistrates:

> Hence it ought to be observed that something remarkable is here demanded from princes, besides an ordinary profession of faith; for the Lord has bestowed on them authority and power to defend the Church and to promote the glory of God. This is indeed the duty of all; but kings, in proportion as their power is greater, ought to devote themselves to it more earnestly, and to labor in it more diligently.

Calvin outlines in specific detail the twofold duty Isaiah requires of "nursing fathers." Calvin insists the kind of "nursing" Isaiah had in mind was, first and foremost, spiritual. A ruler should serve the church by "removing superstitions and putting an end to all wicked idolatry . . . advancing the kingdom of Christ and maintaining purity of doctrine . . . [and] purging scandals and cleansing from the filth that corrupts piety and impairs the luster of the Divine majesty." In summary, a good king ought to use his authority to ensure his subjects worship God the right way.

Kings have a second and equally important responsibility. Spiritual oversight can get expensive. It requires buildings and salaries and programs for providing care to the unfortunate. If kings are to keep the church pure, they must also keep the church doors open. Here's Calvin again:

> Undoubtedly, while kings bestow careful attention on these [spiritual] things, they at the same time supply the pastors and ministers of the Word with all that is necessary for food and maintenance, provide for the poor and guard the Church against the disgrace of pauperism; erect schools, and appoint salaries for the teachers and board for the students; build poor-houses and hospitals, and make every other arrangement that belongs to the protection and defense of the Church.

The twofold duty Calvin outlines for monarchs—encouraging orthodoxy and subsidizing the cost of ministry—defines what it means to be a "nursing father" in far more detail than Isaiah does in chapter 49. To those of us reading from the twenty-first century, it may seem that Calvin chose these two responsibilities arbitrarily. He didn't.

When Calvin writes in other places about the roles and responsibilities of civil government, he prescribes this same twofold duty for monarchs based on a pattern in the Old Testament. In Scripture, Calvin writes, "holy kings are especially praised for restoring worship of God when [that worship is] corrupted or overthrown, or for taking care that religion flourished under them in purity and safety"—all of which involved both spiritual and material oversight. Whether Calvin was right or wrong, Isaiah 49:23 was not a proof text. It was a concise summary of a general biblical pattern that describes the role civil government plays in supporting religion. The term "nursing father" was shorthand already in the 1500s for these two responsibilities.

Thus, the founder of New England's theological vision advocated for state-supported clergy. Furthermore, the "nursing fathers" metaphor appears in one of New England's founding documents. The Cambridge Platform of 1648 provided the framework for Massachusetts society and eventually New England more broadly. The platform mandated that if church members should fail to support their pastors willingly and left the church unable to pay them, "the magistrate is to see that the ministry be duly provided for, as appears from the commanded example of Nehemiah." After all, "The magistrates are *nursing fathers* and nursing mothers" and have a responsibility to promote true religion both spiritually and materially.

For all these reasons, Edward Dorr felt he was on firm footing that Election Day in 1765. Like Calvin before him—and like most New Englanders at the time—Dorr believed the Bible commanded civil government to make sure the church thrived. "If we look into the word of God," Dorr explained,

> we always find, that when a good and religious prince ascended the throne of Israel, religion flourished through the nation, and the worship of God was duly attended everywhere; while on the other hand, when an idolatrous prince reigned, idolatry and wickedness became general among the people.

Godly government always results in flourishing faith, Dorr believed. According to the Old Testament pattern, church and state were distinct but indivisible. "The history of the church, in all ages shows, that when *Moses* [church] and *Aaron* [state] walk hand in hand, things go well: But when the ministers of the state, and of the church, differ and disagree, all things run into confusion."

The way the Congregationalists saw it, those Christians who abandoned established churches in order to form new ones were guilty of violating the first table of the Ten Commandments: they had stopped worshiping properly. Even if they continued to pay taxes to support the local ministry, they would still be violating the spiritual commands. But the Separates were doing more: they were failing to worship properly *and* they refused to support the ministry through taxation. They were in error and needed to be corrected. And if they wouldn't respond to the spiritual authority of New England's ministers, surely they would respond to the civil authority of New England's magistrates.

A New Approach to Scripture

Over the course of his lifetime, Backus argued his case for religious liberty from many angles—from reason, from philosophy, from theology. The firmest foundation for his position remained, in his mind, the clear teaching of the Bible. What is interesting though is that the way Backus interpreted the Bible evolved during the course of his legal battles.

By the 1750s, Backus and his fellow Baptists began experiencing social and political consequences for refusing to pay their taxes. Backus's mother, Elizabeth, was imprisoned in 1752. "She was sick" on the night she was arrested and had wrapped herself in heavy blankets and was sitting near the fire "reading the family Bible." The officer sent to arrest her naively believed that because she was sick and elderly, she'd rather pay the fines than go to jail. "But Mrs. Backus was not the woman to abandon her religious principles," a witness observed. Elizabeth went to jail rather than compromise her scruples. A fellow church member paid her debt.

Experiences like this convinced Backus it was time to start defending his point of view in print. He published his first tract in 1754, called *A Discourse Showing the Nature and Necessity of an*

Internal Call to Preach the Everlasting Gospel. (This was before the age of catchy book titles.) Already in his earliest writings, the Bible was a fundamental source of argument for Backus. In *An Internal Call,* Backus criticized the legal requirements that pastors could be authorized to preach only if they had first received a proper education and were approved by a council of ministers. "Multitudes place their qualifications more in human learning than in divine enlightenment," Backus wrote, "and place their authority more in being externally called and set apart by men than in being internally called by the Spirit of God."

The Bible, by contrast, is full of characters God set apart for a specific work by communicating with them through a personal, internal calling. Prophets such as Ezekiel and leaders such as Moses, Joshua, and the apostle Paul all had remarkable experiences of God's calling. The specifics of these calls were unique and likely not repeatable, Backus admits. God doesn't typically communicate through visions, burning bushes, or blinding light on the roadside. "And yet the essence and nature of [Paul's] conversion, as he describes it himself . . . is the same that all souls in every age must experience, or they can never enter into the Kingdom of God." The Scriptures are as authoritative today as they were then. "What was spoken to any of God's people of old"—that is, to the Israelites in the Old Testament or the church in the New Testament—"as directions or commands to duty is of constant use now to guide his people." God's expectation for human obedience hasn't changed over time. "The same also may be said of the promises."

Catch this—it's a subtle point. In the early 1750s, Backus read the Bible just like Edward Dorr did. He made his case based on a pattern found in Scripture—the consistent elements of a call to ministry. This pattern appeared in both the Old Testament and the New Testament. And Backus, like most other pastors and theologians of his generation, read the Bible as one continuing narrative. The promises God made to Israel in the Old Testament apply to the church in the New Testament.

This approach to the Bible made it hard for him to argue his case for religious liberty. If all God's promises and commands from the Old Testament apply today, why shouldn't the model of state-supported religion found in the Old Testament be replicated today?

Just a couple of years later, Backus started changing the second variable in the interpretive equation. While he still believed the Bible was true and authoritative without exception for the Christian in any age, he started to make clear distinctions between how things worked for Israel in the Old Testament and for the church in the New Testament and beyond. In 1756 he published a pamphlet titled *A Short Description of the Differences Between the Bond-Woman and the Free*, which took its title from Galatians 4:31: "So then, brethren, we are not children of the bondwoman, but of the free." The pamphlet was a defense of believer's baptism, and it is the first evidence that Backus had adopted a new way of interpreting the Bible.

Advocates of infant baptism in the Calvinist tradition taught (and still teach) that baptism is the New Testament sign of God's covenant with his people, just as circumcision was the Old Testament sign of God's covenant with his people. Just as infants born to faithful Israelites were circumcised as a symbol of God's faithfulness to them, so infants born to faithful Christians are baptized as a symbol of the covenant of grace. This way of interpreting Scripture assumes significant continuity between Old Testament Israel and the New Testament church. It assumes that the promises God made to Israel in the Old Testament are fulfilled in the church in the New. It assumes that God works in the church in roughly the same way that he worked among the Israelites.

Over time, Backus came to disagree with this way of thinking. Where Congregationalists saw continuity between the Old Testament and the New, Backus saw discontinuity. The Old Testament was a "covenant of works" that describes "all the ways in particular wherein men seek for life by what they can do, and think, either in whole or in part, to satisfy their sins, and purchase divine favors, either by duties of morality or by observing any ordinances and forms of worship whatsoever." The New Testament, by contrast, is about "the glorious covenant of grace made between the Father and the Son, before the world began." The two could not be more different. Circumcision belonged to the covenant of works. Baptism belongs to the covenant of grace.

Two years before, Backus had argued in print that all the commands and promises of the entire Bible applied to God's children—by which he meant Christians—in every generation. Now he argued, "The promises and threatenings of the old covenant belong *to the children of the old covenant*, and the promises of the new covenant belong only to *her* children"—that is, Christians.

This shift in how Backus read the Bible had several consequences. First it gave him a biblical basis for separation, because it helped him explain his view that a church should be made up only of converted believers. Jesus told a parable about the kingdom of heaven, recorded in Matthew 13:24-30:

> Another parable put he forth unto them, saying, The kingdom of heaven is likened unto a man which sowed good seed in his field:
>
> But while men slept, his enemy came and sowed tares among the wheat, and went his way.
>
> But when the blade was sprung up, and brought forth fruit, then appeared the tares also.
>
> So the servants of the householder came and said unto him, Sir, didst not thou sow good seed in thy field? from whence then hath it tares?
>
> He said unto them, An enemy hath done this. The servants said unto him, Wilt thou then that we go and gather them up?
>
> But he said, Nay; lest while ye gather up the tares, ye root up also the wheat with them.

> Let both grow together until the harvest: and in the time of harvest I will say to the reapers, Gather ye together first the tares, and bind them in bundles to burn them: but gather the wheat into my barn.

Commonly in the eighteenth century, this parable was interpreted to mean that the "field" Jesus is talking about is the church. Ideally the field would contain only good grain (i.e., converted Christians). Nevertheless, it also contains tares or weeds (i.e., unconverted people). Thus, until Jesus comes back at the end of time, the church will be filled with both Christians and non-Christians. There's no sense trying to separate them.

Backus, like other dissenters, interpreted this passage differently. He understood the "field" to represent the "world," not the church. Jesus is explaining here that the church will always be *surrounded* by the wicked—because the church is in the world—not that the church should always *include* the wicked among its members.

Perhaps most significantly, this new way of interpreting the Bible was essential for Backus's understanding of the roles of the church and the civil authority and their relationship to one another. Edward Dorr argued that the Old Testament pattern demanded that the church be supported by civil government. Backus insisted that the example of Israel no longer applied to Christians because that pattern of state-sponsored religion was a relic of the covenant of law, the "bondwoman." Christians live under the covenant of grace. The new covenant calls for a reassessment of the relationship of church and state. It took Backus a little while to work out the details. But by this point he was on his way to formulating a biblical and theological argument for religious liberty.

Tectonic Shift

Interpreting the Bible a new way was a change of perspective for Backus that brought clarity to a number of pressing issues. Emphasizing the discontinuity between Israel and the New Testament church gave Backus the framework he needed to defend his separation from the Standing Order church. It gave him firm footing to reject infant baptism. And it became the linchpin in his biblical argument against religious taxation. Ultimately, the shift enabled Backus to articulate the relationship between the church and the broader culture. The church should exist for the good of the culture. But in order to function as a pure and true church, it had to relinquish formal power and risk sacrificing influence.

I was born at the beginning of the Reagan era. The previous president, Jimmy Carter, was the first American president to refer to himself as "born again." He talked like an evangelical insider. He told supporters, "I believe God wants me to be the best politician I can be." His election validated evangelicalism in American public life and inspired other evangelicals, including Pat Robertson, to aspire to political influence. Carter ultimately disappointed many evangelicals, but not before he catalyzed them to pursue positions of cultural influence through politics.

Ronald Reagan was different. Reagan did more than speak the evangelical dialect. He championed evangelical causes. He was the first president to speak at the annual gathering of the National Association of Evangelicals. He openly opposed abortion and championed "family values." More strategically, perhaps, he staffed influential government positions with Christians and appointed federal judges who were sympathetic to evangelical causes.

The rise of politically influential evangelicals and their movements—the Moral Majority, the religious right, the Christian Coalition—made many evangelicals hopeful of moving from the margins of American culture into the mainstream. It gave them a new vision of a godly America in which the nation's laws and the people's morals were shaped by the Word of God. This vision has never been fully realized. However, for nearly the last twenty years, evangelicals have made up a critical voting bloc. It is difficult to become president without winning the evangelical vote. It is difficult to win the evangelical vote without championing evangelical causes. The movement has enjoyed a long season of social clout and national influence.

Precisely because of this influence and how it has been stewarded, evangelical influence is waning in America. Christians and non-Christians view this waning influence in different ways. One 2016 survey concluded that nearly 80 percent of "white evangelical Protestants say that discrimination against

Christians now rivals that of other groups." At the same time, nearly 80 percent of "religiously unaffiliated Americans and adherents of non-Christian religions" *disagree* that American Christians experience greater discrimination than other groups.

I can't help but wonder if what some evangelicals interpret as discrimination, or even persecution, is actually loss of influence. Perhaps what feels like loss of liberty is actually loss of power or privilege. In previous generations, many evangelicals assumed the American government should support and incentivize Christian morality, worship, and practice. From tax-exempt status to definitions of marriage, the state should reinforce Christian values. If we view this arrangement as our *due*, we are sure to be disappointed when the relationship changes.

If, however, one believes with Backus and his fellow Baptists that true piety might require sacrificing influence, that the Christian's calling is not to halls of power but to fellowship with the marginalized—from that perspective, changes in the nation's posture toward evangelicalism seem hardly strange at all. We should absolutely resist actual loss of liberty not only for ourselves but also for others. Loss of privilege, however, may be unavoidable. It might even be good for us.

If creating a culture of faithful disagreement is a first priority as we consider religious liberty, a second priority must be determining how we understand the relationship between the church and the broader culture.

—~—

Backus recognized and embraced his status on the margins. But as a citizen in a nation of laws, he was motivated to take decisive action to secure religious liberty. In the years to come, Backus's understanding of Scripture and the church developed into a more organized resistance.

FIVE

A RECORD OF WRONGS

In civil states particular men are invested with authority to judge for the whole; but in Christ's kingdom each one has an equal right to judge for himself. . . . Christ will have no pressed soldiers in his army.

Isaac Backus, *A Fish Caught in His Own Net*

Baptists did their best in eighteenth-century America to work within the law as they started new churches and baptized new believers. Sometimes they had to be creative.

The certificate law required new Baptist churches to receive endorsements from three Old Baptist churches, churches that were identified as Baptist before the Great Awakening. Fortunately for the new Baptists, the local magistrates didn't always know which congregations were old and which were new. To satisfy the certificate law, then, many new Baptist congregations endorsed one another when Old Baptist congregations refused to lend a hand. In this way and others, the Baptists began to recognize their strength in numbers and the value of healthy collaboration.

As the number of Baptists and Baptist congregations grew in the eighteenth century, they were forced to address challenges both in the long term and in the short term. One of the more damning charges against Baptist ministers was that they were, for the most part, uneducated. Without an education, Baptist clergy suffered from a lack of respectability. The trouble was, they couldn't stomach studying at any of New England's institutions of higher learning. Many feared the professors at those schools—and indeed many of the pastors those schools produced—were unregenerate sinners who stubbornly refused to recognize God's work in the Awakening.

Backus, for his part, was quick to clarify that he was no "enemy to learning," as some of his critics charged. What he objected to was "some sorts of learning" that he considered typical of the New England colleges. Learning of these sorts included "the art of disputing against the truth" and "the art of making easy things hard instead of hard things easy." He was troubled, too, that the colleges were graduating young men for ministry who lacked a biblical understanding of the human condition and the need for personal regeneration. Of these young graduates Backus observed, "It is too notorious to be denied that many scholars that have come out of college of late are rank Arminians."

Baptists needed education and couldn't trust the existing institutions. There was only one thing to do: they joined forces to found a college specifically for training Baptist pastors. The College of Rhode Island, later renamed Brown University, was the first Baptist institution of higher education in America. Isaac Backus did not found the college, but he was a member of its first board of trustees, a position he occupied for thirty-five years.

Incorporating new churches and establishing institutions may have contributed to the long-term success of Baptists in America, but those efforts did not address immediate challenges. Increasing numbers of Baptists faced renewed opposition from local ministers and civil officials. Laws put in place to protect Baptist worship were sometimes ignored. The Baptists needed an advocate.

Liberty of Conscience

In his first efforts to persuade leading officials that dissenters should be free from civil consequences for religious matters, Backus tried to leverage a value he shared with New England Congregationalists: liberty of conscience. Backus believed the primary reason the founding fathers "both of Plymouth and Boston" sought the New World was to experience "a reformation according to the word of God." To experience this reformation, the founders of New England were willing to break with tradition and embrace new ways of thinking if they were convinced the Scriptures led them in a particular direction. The spiritual fathers of New England "covenanted before God to embrace further light from his word as it should be opened to them."

Being open to "further light" didn't mean throwing off all limitations and being free to believe whatever they liked. "Further light" wasn't *new* revelation. It was a fresh awareness or deeper understanding of what God's Word had always meant but that, for whatever reason, people had been unable to see. It was throwing off the blinders to embrace God's truth anew.

The thing is, people sometimes received "further light" from God's Word to varying degrees and at different times. This meant people had to be free to accept as truth what the Holy Spirit convinced them of through the Scriptures. You and I may disagree, but we should be free to disagree. This was liberty of conscience. It was the duty of every believer to follow Scripture rather than tradition where the two parted ways. New England's founders understood this, Backus argued, and made it a point of doctrine to test all truth by Scripture. The responsibility to test all truth by Scripture implies every individual has the freedom to judge the truth for him- or herself.

In some of his early writings, Backus seemed confident he could convince the Standing Order to recognize Baptist convictions about baptism (for example) as a case of "further light" from Scripture. Baptists weren't innovating a new interpretation of the Bible, Backus argued. Instead, their eyes had finally been opened to a truth that had always been there but that many had been unable to see. While Baptists and Congregationalists may disagree about how to interpret the Bible, surely they could agree to the importance of protecting the liberty of a person's conscience to follow the Holy Spirit. Backus's opponents didn't see things this way. Not only did the Standing Order reject the Baptist understanding of biblical baptism, they also rejected Backus's understanding of liberty of conscience.

On one occasion Backus wrote a letter to the minister who censured Abraham and Elizabeth Lord. Abraham Lord stopped attending the Congregational church because the church practiced a variation on the Half-Way Covenant by baptizing the children of church members who hadn't given testimony of faith. Overall, Abraham sensed a general "spirit of opposition against the Spirit of God in the church." Abraham and Elizabeth claimed that continuing to worship in this congregation would cause them to sin against their conscience.

The minister of the church refused to let them leave. He judged their reasons for leaving to be insufficient. As long as the Lords were members of the Congregational church, they were subject to the leadership of the church. Since Abraham and Elizabeth were not permitted to leave the church, they were still considered members. But because they had been absent from worship for a while, the pastor pronounced the couple under church discipline for neglecting the Lord's Supper. Though they didn't want to be members at all, they now were being punished for being *bad* members.

The Lords were perplexed about how to proceed. They wrote their minister a formal request to withdraw from membership so they could join the local Baptist church. The minister refused to let them break membership, on the grounds that "nothing but very weighty and grievous things lying upon the conscience, which they cannot remedy, can justify a person to separate" from their church. The pastor's response is remarkable because it concedes the point that a matter of conscience *should* be a reason to break fellowship. He simply wasn't convinced that *these* matters were "weighty and grievous" enough to count as matters of conscience.

The minister's response becomes more remarkable still. The minister went on to say that he had his own conscience to think about. "Liberty of conscience we claim ourselves," he wrote, "and allow others as a darling point." But the minister claimed that letting members leave the church would cause *him* to sin against his own conscience because doing so would require him to knowingly allow them to commit a theological error.

This feels like an example of making easy things hard instead of making hard things easy.

At this point of impasse, Backus came to the couple's defense. Backus had baptized Abraham and Elizabeth, and he felt an obligation to take up their fight. His primary point of contention was that the Standing Order churches violated liberty of conscience by reserving the right to decide what issues were serious enough to justify separation. "If it is only the *church* that is to judge," Backus argued, "then where is their allowance of liberty to others as a darling point?" In Backus's opinion, the Standing Order bound Baptist consciences by not permitting them to worship in whatever church they deemed right.

Backus was threading a theological needle here. He acknowledged the authority of a true church to discipline its members.

A member of his *own* church who fell into sin, for example, would be subject to church discipline. The way Backus saw it, though, the Congregational churches had deviated from Scripture by practicing infant baptism. They had deviated from Scripture *and tradition* by admitting members without a profession of faith. Thus they had ceased to be true, biblical churches. They had lost their spiritual authority. They had no authority to discipline members. Dissenters were within their rights to appeal to conscience and leave such churches.

Backus believed staying in a Congregational church caused believers to sin against their consciences, because staying required them to ignore or deny the truth the Holy Spirit revealed to them through the Word of God. The Standing Order didn't see it this way. When people tried to leave with the minister's blessing (letting them out of the covenant), the minister claimed that his conscience wouldn't allow it. If people left anyway, they were disciplined by the civil authorities. This left dissenters with an impossible choice. Either they could stay in the church and sin against their conscience, or they could leave the church and risk civil punishment. Ultimately, Backus wanted to convince Standing Order pastors to acknowledge liberty of conscience as a sufficient reason to leave a church without fear of reprisal from civil authorities.

The fundamental issue for Backus was sovereignty. Only the Scriptures had a right to claim sovereignty—supreme authority—over the conscience, but in practice the Standing Order claimed sovereignty over the consciences of dissenters.

Of course, Backus knew humans are prone to error, so those who claimed "further light" should have to make a case for it. He understood that breaking with the standing churches would require apologetics. His hope was that "when we have delivered our sentiments and the grounds of them, then to say with Paul, Judge ye what I say." Unfortunately the Standing Order did not often respond with spirited debate. Instead of engaging in dialogue, the Standing Order sent the magistrate to arrest the wrongdoers.

The "finishing stroke" for Backus was "for the secular arm to finish what the church has begun." For all practical purposes, there was no separation of church and state. "The church has declared the Baptist to be irregular, therefore the secular power still forces them to support the worship which they conscientiously object from."

There was a great irony in all of this, Backus was no doubt pleased to point out. With their lax rules about church membership, the Standing Order would let just about anyone *into* the church. With their narrow understanding of liberty of conscience, they refused to let anyone *out* of the church. The ministers worried themselves very little about who was eligible for membership. But when members dissented, they were quick to exert their authority for discipline.

Backus and the Baptists harped on religious taxes because taxation was the most concrete evidence of an establishment of religion in New England. But taxation wasn't the root of the problem. The root of the problem, and what was more fundamentally disturbing to Backus, was that taxation implied sovereignty. The tax was evidence that the Standing Order believed they had the authority to levy taxes. The amount wasn't the issue. "It is not the pence but the power, that alarms us." That was why Backus rejected the certificate system. Filing a certificate would have gotten him out of the tax. But filing a certificate would have forced Backus to acknowledge that the Standing Order had both the authority to tax and the authority to exempt from taxation. Backus denied them this authority.

Baptists didn't have many options. Many left their Congregational or Separate churches, joined Baptist congregations, and prepared themselves to face the consequences. An episode in Ashfield, Massachusetts, illustrates just how much it could cost to stand on principle.

Life, Liberty, and Property

The story of Baptist persecution in Ashfield, Massachusetts, is complicated. Here are the salient points.

One of the first settlers of Ashfield was a man named Chileab Smith. He became a New Light during the Awakening, and his move to Ashfield allowed him an excuse to leave his Congregational church. In those early days, Ashfield had no church, and Smith's son felt a call to ministry. So the Smiths formed a congregation of Baptists and built a meetinghouse in 1761.

The town was predominately Baptist for the first seven years it existed, in part because the locals scuffled with Native American tribes for those seven years and new inhabitants were slow to move in during seasons of armed conflict. During that time, the Baptists in Ashfield enjoyed freedom to worship as they pleased and freedom from religious taxation. That changed when the conflict with neighboring Native Americans ended. Once the threat of war passed, new settlers streamed in and the town grew. Baptists soon lost their majority status in Ashfield, and local tax assessors seized the opportunity to start levying taxes against them. Assessors charged that the Baptists had not founded the church properly because—you guessed it—the pastor of the church, Chileab Smith's son, had not been properly educated, nor had he been ordained by a council of Congregational ministers.

The regional court agreed, and the locals appointed a Congregational pastor for the town, a man named Jacob Sherwin. The new pastor's appointment came with a generous resettlement package, an annual salary, and the commitment of a lump sum to build a meetinghouse. To raise the necessary capital for all these expenses, the court taxed the Baptists.

At first the Baptists played by the rules. They paid the taxes, grudgingly, while they consistently advocated for their own rights in court. Instead of ruling in their favor, the court levied *more* taxes on the Baptists, adding property taxes to the existing poll taxes. At this point, the Baptist citizens of Ashfield had had enough. In a courageous act of protest, they refused to pay the taxes they owed. They opted for civil disobedience.

With that, legislative opposition turned to open persecution. Constables seized private property from Baptist landowners and sold it for pennies on the dollar to cover the sum of unpaid ecclesiastical taxes and fines they owed. Nearly four hundred acres of land, valued at "three hundred and sixty-three pounds thirteen shillings, lawful money," were confiscated and sold at auction for "nineteen pounds three shillings." If the loss of land and money were not enough, the property included a cemetery in which family members of the local Baptists were buried. As one citizen put it, not only had the government taken their land, "they have taken from us our dead." One family operated an apple orchard on the parcel. Officials uprooted all the apple trees and tore down the fences. These actions were clearly intended not only to recover lost tax revenue but to send a clear message that dissenters belong under the thumb of the magistrate.

Incidents like these galvanized the Baptists of the region for action. It took dramatic opposition to force them to do it, but they decided to organize. The Baptist movement from the beginning had been the activity of a growing number of largely unrelated churches and pastors who were happy to support and encourage one another. This collaborative spirit is what motivated the young Isaac Backus to itinerate around the region to preach. But concerns about the liberty of the individual conscience meant that individuals and their congregations remained quite autonomous. Even within congregations, Baptists were hesitant to submit their own consciences to the rule of others. For this reason, they were suspicious of centralizing authority in the form of a denomination or, worse yet, a "presbytery." Presbyterianism—at least in regard to their form of church governance—was a slippery slope to a papacy, as far as many Baptists were concerned. Even those Baptists who were most committed to fostering deep relationships among Baptist congregations, Isaac Backus chief among them, were hesitant to organize in such a way that wrenched decision-making power away from local congregations and gave it to a larger, central governing body.

Even so, episodes such as the persecution in Ashfield convinced Baptists that they were stronger together than apart. They were certainly open to sharing one another's burdens and collaborating to battle unjust legislation. By 1767, Backus and others were convinced that some form of organization was essential to the Baptists' long-term success. They formed the Warren Association with the purpose of providing one another with financial, spiritual, and moral support.

Ultimately the Warren Association helped the Baptists in Ashfield secure the tax exemption that was their legal right. In August 1769, a subcommittee of the association, known as the Grievance Committee, published an advertisement in a popular Boston newspaper calling for any and all Baptists in New England "who are or have been oppressed in any way on a religious account" to prepare a testimony of their oppression. The appeal was personal and compelling:

> It would be needless to tell you that you have long felt the effects of the laws by which the religion of the government in which you live is established. Your purses have felt the

> burden of ministerial rates; and when these would not satisfy your enemies, your property hath been taken from you and sold for less than half its value. These things you cannot forget. You will therefore readily hear and attend, when you are desired to collect your cases of suffering and have them well attested.

Simple stories wouldn't do. They had to be "well attested." The committee called on Baptists to collect hard evidence of abuse, including "the taxes you have paid to build meeting-houses, to settle ministers, and support them, with all the time, money, and labor you have lost in waiting on courts, seeing lawyers, etc."

Churches and individuals responded with gusto. The Grievance Committee received many dozens of well-documented reports verifying that the exemption laws in place in New England were being either misapplied or outright ignored across the region. The ultimate goal of the Grievance Committee was to compile these irrefutable stories of oppression into something like Foxe's *Book of Martyrs*. They wanted to put these stories in front of every magistrate and councilman in New England until someone could no longer deny the complaints of Baptists throughout the region and was motivated to rule in their favor.

Isaac Backus was one of the Grievance Committee's most effective and efficient members. When he and the other committee members had collected accounts of abuse and oppression from across New England, they published an impassioned letter to the Massachusetts General Court asking that the state to repay Baptists for damages incurred in the form of taxes, fines, fees, and confiscated property; that Baptists be permanently exempted from religious taxes in New England; and that the injustices in Ashfield specifically should be made right. The first two demands were never met. But the General Court did overrule local legislation that was especially onerous for Ashfield Baptists.

It was his leadership in the Grievance Committee effort that earned Backus a place of prominence in the Warren Association and among the churches of the region. In 1772, the Baptists of Massachusetts nominated Backus to be their representative—they called him "the agent for the Baptists in New England"—and they put him in a position to serve Baptists throughout New England by appointing him chairman of the Warren Association's Grievance Committee.

Civil Disobedience

As chairman of the Grievance Committee, Backus aimed to replicate his efforts on behalf of the brothers in Ashfield on a larger scale. New England's legislators routinely downplayed the plight of Baptists.

First, they maintained that while Baptists might be miffed about having to pay religious taxes, their treatment certainly did not amount to oppression. Were they inconvenienced? Maybe. But surely they were not persecuted.

Second, on the rare occasion that a legislative body admitted outright persecution against dissenters of any sort, they insisted that the mistreatment was local and occasional. There was no colony-wide policy of injustice against Baptists that made special legislation necessary. Persecution was the work of a few bad eggs, not evidence of systemic problems.

To counter these objections, Backus aimed to gather overwhelming and irrefutable evidence of systemic, colony-wide persecution against religious dissenters. The Warren Association provided the vast and formal network through which to communicate stories from the front line. The Grievance Committee's work on behalf of Ashfield established precedent that an effort like this could succeed. The objective now was to demonstrate a pattern of abuse, to document it, and to publicize it.

The longer Backus searched, the more evidence he found. Some gave accounts of seized property and imprisonment. Others like Martha Kimball, a widow from Bradford, were treated shamefully even when they complied with the assessor's demands. Ms. Kimball was charged a ministerial tax, even though she was a registered Baptist with a certificate on file in the collector's office. She wrote to Backus: "This is to let you know that in the year 1768, in a very cold night in the winter, about nine or ten o'clock in the evening, I was taken prisoner and carried, by the collector in the town where I live, from my family, consisting of three small children in order to be put into jail."

Because the night was cold, she convinced her captors to take a short break at a tavern by the road. There they held her for several hours, until she finally agreed to pay the tax—a tax from which she was legally exempt. In a postscript, Ms. Kimball added, "It may be observed that the tavern whither they took me is about two miles from my house. After I paid what they demanded, then I had to return to my poor fatherless children through the snow, on foot, in the dead of night, exposed to the severity of the cold." No doubt this story struck a chord with Backus. Something very similar had happened to his mother more than a decade before.

Backus spent months collecting narratives of abuse like this one, verifying the claims by cross-checking town records, interviewing Congregational clergy, and visiting the affected pastors, members, and churches. He even had his own experiences to include in his accounts. His mother and brother had both been imprisoned for refusing to pay ecclesiastical taxes, and Backus himself had been arrested a number of times, though his bond was always paid by fellow Baptists. The more stories he collected, the less confident Backus became that any amount of evidence would ever be enough to convince his opponents. The time had come to take more radical measures. Backus wanted to leverage his growing network of well-connected and well-funded Baptists to launch a campaign of colony-wide civil disobedience.

Before a meeting of the Warren Association, Backus presented his plan. Baptists across New England—all of them—must refuse to pay the taxes their local assessors claimed they owe. When forced to choose between payment or prison, Baptists must choose prison en masse. Imprisoned Baptists would fill the local jails to overflowing. This would prove the breadth of abuse Baptists were subjected to. Their solidarity in the face of persecution would prove the sincerity of their cause. Officials would have no grounds to claim that Baptists resisted taxation simply for financial reasons. It was certainly simpler to pay the taxes than to go to jail. Moreover, if the colony's jails were suddenly full of committed Baptists, officials would have no grounds to claim that injustices against Baptists were rare and isolated incidents. Civil disobedience, Backus believed, was the only sure strategy for securing the liberty he and his fellow Baptists desired.

Whether or not he was right, we will never know. The audience present at the association meeting agreed in theory with Backus's proposal. A coordinated act of civil disobedience would almost certainly *work*. Unfortunately, the association wasn't in a position to mandate the action. Every local church and every individual member within each church was free to act as they chose—free to follow their conscience. The association could only recommend and advise participation. It couldn't compel anyone to comply. Partial participation pulled most of the teeth from the threat of civil disobedience. Everyone present recognized that. As something of a consolation, the Warren Association committed financial support to anyone who chose jail time over taxes. Whatever fees and fines those people incurred, the Warren Association would pay for.

Backus resigned himself to battle with the pen. He continued to compose tracts and pamphlets, to preach sermons and campaign before local magistrates and Standing Order ministers. He chose, too, to demonstrate the universality of the Baptist predicament and the solidarity of their beliefs by undertaking a massive writing project, a multivolume history of Baptists in America that chronicled the beliefs and experiences of Baptists and other dissenters in New England from the Plymouth Pilgrims to Backus's own day.

Meanwhile, America was edging ever nearer to all-out war with Mother England. As that day approached, Backus found a way to bring the Baptist cause into the national limelight.

SIX

RELIGIOUS LIBERTY ON THE EVE OF WAR

The care of souls cannot belong to the civil magistrate, because his power consists only in outward force; but pure and saving religion consists in the inward persuasion of the mind, without which nothing can be acceptable to God.

Isaac Backus to the Massachusetts delegates to the First Continental Congress

The American Revolution provided an interesting opportunity for advocates of religious liberty.

In 1774, tensions between England and the American colonies were formalizing into conflict. Delegates from twelve of the thirteen colonies met in Philadelphia to discuss possible responses to the so-called Intolerable Acts. America was on the eve of war, and its citizens were prepared to protect liberty and the right of self-governance at any cost.

One beef the colonists had with England had to do with taxation without representation. Many Baptists, including Isaac Backus, believed the growing American disdain for taxation meant the cultural tide was shifting. Hadn't the Baptists been objecting to religious taxation without spiritual representation for the last twenty years? Perhaps the Baptists' countrymen were finally coming around.

The Baptists chose what they considered an opportune moment to move their struggle for freedom beyond the local level by associating it directly with the colonies' fight for freedom in general. The Baptists were sure the men gathered in Philadelphia for the Continental Congress were predisposed to take up the cause of the oppressed. They needed to get their argument for religious liberty, and their account of the injustices they'd suffered, in front of those delegates if they had any chance at all of securing additional legal protection.

Instead of meeting with all fifty-six delegates, the Baptists decided to make their case before the delegates from Massachusetts only. This group included Thomas Cushing, Samuel Adams, John Adams, and Robert Treat Paine. And instead of descending on Philadelphia en masse, the Baptists of New England opted to send a delegate on their behalf. An association of twenty Baptist churches convened outside of Boston on September 14, 1774, and unanimously selected Isaac Backus to plead their case in front of the Massachusetts delegates to the Continental Congress.

Backus shared with the delegates a long-prepared statement, approved by his sending churches. It delineated the weaknesses of the legislation currently in place to protect religious liberty in Massachusetts and beyond. He recounted stories of injustice. And he distributed copies of his most famous tract, *An Appeal to the Public for Religious Liberty*.

A Theology of Liberty and Government

Backus published *An Appeal to the Public for Religious Liberty* the year before the Congress, in 1773. It was his manifesto as agent for the Baptists in New England. Backus had proposed a campaign of widespread civil disobedience. By patiently enduring the persecution that would inevitably result when Baptists refused to support the Standing Order clergy or make use of the certificate exemption, Backus hoped to sway the religious establishment and win the favor of the public. *Appeal to the Public* was a key part of this strategy. It articulated his views of the state and the church, their relationship to each other, and the sanctity of the individual conscience. Backus's fellow Baptists decided against civil disobedience. But they supported *Appeal to the Public* as their official statement of protest.

Backus's purpose for the tract was modest. He proposed to "offer a few thoughts concerning the general nature of liberty and government, and then shew [*sic*] wherein it appears to us, that our religious rights are encroached upon in this land." But instead of simply offering a "few thoughts," he advanced a compelling argument that at the core of America's liberty problem there was actually a theological problem.

Government, Backus began, was essential to human liberty. He defined "true human liberty" as "to know, obey, and enjoy his Creator and to do all the good unto, and enjoy all the happiness with and in, his fellow creatures that he is capable of." In the Garden of Eden, Adam and Eve enjoyed this perfect liberty under the direct supervision—or *government*—of God. The first humans did not imagine that "submission to government and acting strictly by rule was confinement." Rather they happily followed "the authority of Heaven." Their trouble started when they separated liberty and government, when they believed the serpent's lie that they could only experience true freedom outside of God's limitations. In this way, "man first lost his freedom by breaking over the rules of government." The social consequences of this rebellion were swift and severe. Adam had

> no sooner revolted from the authority of Heaven than the beauty and order of his family was broken. He turns accuser against the wife of his bosom, his first son murders the next, and then lies to his Master to conceal it, and that lying murderer's posterity were the first who broke over the order of marriage which God had instituted.

Adam and Eve did not experience greater liberty when they overthrew their government. Instead, they became slaves of sin, death, and chaos. And the trouble didn't end with them. It spread. Like a genetic mutation (my metaphor, not Backus's), that chaos has been transferred from generation to generation. Ever since Adam sinned, Backus explained, humanity has been plagued with a "dreadful distemper" that seeks liberty outside the confines of government of all sorts. People seek spiritual freedom outside of God's commands. They seek social freedom outside the bounds of civil government. The result, of course, is that true freedom is now beyond our grasp.

Backus was no doomsday prophet. He didn't believe things would inevitably get worse until the second coming. He believed order could be restored. But he was clear that could only happen if people once again recognized where true freedom comes from: knowing one's place before God and one's obligations to him and to one's neighbor. Things will never return to their pre-fall, Garden-of-Eden conditions. Rather than walking with folks in the cool of the evening, God now mediates his rule (government) through two earthly entities: the state and the church.

Civil government (the state) has as its jurisdiction the safety of people's bodies. Civil government prevents people from killing or stealing. It maintains social order and preserves the peace. Civil government is certainly necessary, then. But it is not sufficient for restoring human liberty to its fullness.

Ecclesiastical government (the church), by contrast, is concerned with the state of people's souls. Because Backus believed that humans lost their true liberty in the act of rebellion against God, he also believed true liberty could be restored only when humans once again submitted to God's governance. He didn't place his ultimate hope for human freedom in legislation. Instead Backus put his hope in spiritual regeneration, which realigns the human will with the divine will. For Backus, the greatest threat to liberty that humans face is "soul slavery." And no human government can relieve that bondage; "'tis only the power of the Gospel that can set them free from sin so as to become the servants of righteousness."

This is a major departure from New England's dominant understanding of church and state. There was no room for "nursing fathers" in Backus's view of government. He spent the first full section of his presentation making this clear.

Once Backus had established the different roles and responsibilities of the church and the state, he spent the second section of *Appeal to the Public* identifying three ways in which civil and ecclesiastical governments had been conflated and confused in Massachusetts. First, legislation essentially mandated "a pedobaptist worship"—that is, a form of church that practices infant baptism—in every commonwealth. Second, the state held the power to enforce the selection of clergy. And finally, the state supported Congregational clergy by general taxation. These issues together form the heart of Backus's objection to state-organized religious expression. It was through infant baptism, performed by a state approved clergy, who were supported by taxation of all citizens, that the Standing Order maintained its influence over Massachusetts.

From his earliest published works Backus identified the connection between infant baptism and religious establishment. In his letter to his former pastor in 1764, he explained that the founders of New England maintained the separation of church and state even while they professed infant baptism. "Indeed they were not aware," Backus lamented, "that infant baptism laid the foundation of a national church." Perhaps because he had addressed the issue at such great length elsewhere, Backus dedicated the least space in *Appeal to the Public* to pedobaptism, saying only that "it is well known, that infant baptism is never expressed in the Bible, [but] only is upheld by men's reasonings."

He writes at slightly greater length about clergy selection. According to Massachusetts' legislature, the authorities maintained the power to require each new commonwealth to call a minister. What bothered Backus more was that they also reserved the right to determine which ministers were qualified to fill the new pulpits. An eligible clergyman "must be one who has either an academical [*sic*] degree, or a testimonial in his favor from a majority of the ministers in the county where the parish lies." This meant that men the Holy Spirit had gifted for ministry could be refused the opportunity to exercise those gifts if they did not have the proper education or were not approved by a council of Standing Order ministers.

Backus spent the bulk of section two discussing his opposition to religious taxation. As he did with pedobaptism and minister selection, Backus first attacked the practice on exegetical grounds. Appealing to 1 Corinthians 9:13-14 and Galatians 6:6-7, he argued that "the Lord hath ordained that they which preach the Gospel shall live of the Gospel or by the free communications to them which his Gospel will produce." But instead of living by the gospel, "the ministers of our land have chosen to live by the law." This made clergy of the Standing Order the "king's minister[s]," rather than Christ's.

The Heart of the Matter

At the heart of Backus's argument was a clear indictment of human nature. Backus believed people were ignorant about "what we are and where we are." What we are, Backus believed, is selfish, fallen sinners. Where we are is east of Eden, where the selfishness of the majority can enslave a minority group or groups.

The state-supported church, Backus argued, is run by people who are afflicted with the same "disposition," that "dreadful distemper" we all inherited when Adam and Eve sinned. Everyone is now in a "state of revolt" against God's will. Like all people (especially people who have not been born again), the councilmen who appointed pastors in New England were motivated by self-interest. The civil system of religious establishment incentivized the Standing Order to perpetuate its power over spiritual matters. Jonathan Edwards had written years before in a book called *Freedom of the Will* that "the will is as the greatest apparent good is." By this he meant that a person chooses at any given moment to take whatever course of action seems most desirable at the time. It's why an alcoholic drinks, Edwards said—he *chooses* to drink because alcohol is what seems best to him at the moment of decision.

Backus applied the same logic to religious establishment. The self-interest of the electing ministers would never allow them to approve a pastor of another denomination. The greatest apparent good would always be their own comfort and control. "In our dispute about religious liberty," Backus explained, "we must take into consideration, that it is against the interest of the people we apply to, to grant us any remedy." This is human nature. All of us are inclined to want the things we consider best for us.

This natural tendency becomes systemic injustice when laws protect the self-interest of one group at the expense of the rights of others. In Backus's New England, there was no legal recourse for religious minorities. The only group that enjoyed the free exercise of its will was the Standing Order. Backus had essentially given up convincing Standing Order ministers to allow Baptists and others to worship freely. He was now convinced they would never grant that permission. Why would they? It was in their best interest not to. Original sin had rendered their hearts incapable of anything but self-interest.

The Baptists needed a solution that limited the power of one group's self-interest. They needed legislation to protect religious liberty because they couldn't count on their opponents to grant it out of the goodness of their hearts.

To summarize, here's how Backus framed the problem: The spiritual leadership of the whole Massachusetts population was determined by a body of Congregational ministers in whose best interest it was to muffle the voices of dissenters by refusing to ordain ministers of other Protestant denominations. Under the current legislation the more Congregationalists there were in town, the less each citizen had to pay in taxes to cover the minister's salary. It was, therefore, in everyone's best interest to stunt the growth of dissenting groups. For Backus, this made "the majority of the people the test of orthodoxy. For though their laws call them 'orthodox ministers,' yet the grand test of their orthodoxy is the major vote of the people be they saints or sinners, believers or unbelievers."

Because the Standing Order refused to grant liberty of conscience, it had to be protected by legislation.

Before 1773, Backus wrote primarily as a pastor to other pastors appealing to Scripture and history to persuade the establishment to willingly acknowledge the spiritual legitimacy of Separates and Baptists. By 1773 it had become clear to him that the Standing Order had too much to lose to voluntarily allow Baptists liberty of conscience. In other words, by 1773 Backus recognized a political application of one of his core theological beliefs. Backus believed that the natural orientation of humans is always *away* from God. "The grand contest ever since sin entered into the world," wrote Backus in another tract in the same year, "has been between the will of the Creator and the will of the creature." Because of this, civil government is necessary to mitigate human self-interest. Thus, in Backus's mind, the fundamental reason for separation of church and state was not pragmatic or philosophical. It was theological. State-enforced religious liberty ensures that the marginalized are not at the mercy of the fallen human nature of the majority.

This is the theological presentation Backus made to the Massachusetts delegates to the Continental Congress in 1774. He ended his presentation with a clear and compelling request for liberty:

> It may now be asked—*What is the liberty desired?* The answer is; as the kingdom of Christ is not of this world, and religion is a concern between God and the soul with which no human authority can intermeddle; consistently with the principles of Christianity, and according to the dictates of Protestantism, we claim and expect the liberty of worshipping God according to our consciences, not being obliged to support a ministry we cannot attend, whilst we demean ourselves as faithful subjects. These we have an undoubted right to, as men, as Christians, and by charter as inhabitants of Massachusetts Bay.

It's not entirely clear to me what Backus expected to happen at this point. Whatever he hoped for, the delegates' response fell short of Backus's expectations. "The delegates from Massachusetts used all their arts," Backus later recalled, "to represent that we complained without reason." Both Samuel Adams and John Adams made long speeches in which they acknowledged that Massachusetts had an established church, but just barely—"a very slender one, hardly to be called an establishment." Samuel Adams insinuated more than once that the complaints presented came from radicals "who made it a merit to suffer persecution." Paine dismissed the entire issue out of hand by saying that none of it had to do with conscience; it was just about getting out of paying a little money. If the gentlemen would kindly leave their names on a list on their way out, he'd gladly exempt them from taxes. Backus stood on principle. He insisted before he left that the entire issue was most certainly a matter of conscience. Paying the tax or obtaining the necessary certificate to be exempted from the tax acknowledged that human beings have authority over others to evaluate their religious beliefs.

The delegates thanked Backus and his attendants for their time and assured them they would do everything in their power to help.

The Right Argument for the Wrong Audience

Backus correctly grounded his argument for religious liberty in theology. This is a true gift for fellow Christians. Especially for modern Christians who are pulled to pledge allegiance to a particular political party or philosophy, a theological framework for understanding religious liberty is essential. Backus gave his fellow Baptists a shared vocabulary for understanding the heart of the issue. We need the same thing today.

Original sin, the human heart condition Backus describes in *Appeal to the Public*, seems to me a great place to start developing a shared vocabulary about religious liberty. Backus would probably argue that all societal problems have their root in human selfishness broadly defined. Inequities in education and income distribution derive from human self-interest to keep the best for ourselves. Racism stems from fear of the other, and racist policies provide a desired sense of security. People want what appears best to them at the time. What's best *for* me will always seem most important *to* me. Surely our conversations about liberty would be more fruitful if we admitted from the beginning that deep in our core we all want what seems best to us.

What Backus got wrong before the Continental Congress was his audience. Two worlds collided at the Continental Congress. Backus had fought for decades with opponents who were churchmen and theologians. His *Appeal to the Public* is a powerful and nuanced argument for religious liberty. He engages contemporary political philosophy (a very little bit), Scripture, and the Christian tradition. But the presentation was tailored to a different audience from the one seated before him at the Congress. They weren't theologians, and the presentation didn't move them to action. The presentation had been carefully crafted for insiders. But it was presented to outsiders.

To make any progress in debates and discussions about religious liberty, we have to figure out how to have the conversations in the *lingua franca* of the modern political system. This is especially true when the appeal for religious liberty today is perceived as a cover for misogyny, racism, or homophobia. Appeals to Scripture and the Christian tradition become shrill when the hearer doesn't speak the language. In other words, original sin may be a helpful concept for understanding religious liberty within the family of faith. But the concept will likely come across as tone deaf in the broader culture. Advocating for our own religious liberty—and defending the rights of others—requires the mental agility to have the conversation differently with insiders and outsiders.

—∞—

Efforts at the Continental Congress meeting were not entirely fruitless. John Hancock, president of the Congress and eventual signer of the Declaration of Independence, read the material Backus left behind and wrote Backus to say that "the establishment of civil and religious liberty to each denomination in the province, is the sincere wish of this Congress." Unfortunately, the Congress at that time in history had no legislative authority, no real powers of civil government at all. The day would come, Hancock promised, when "this petition," Backus's compelling appeal for religious liberty, "will most certainly meet with all that attention due to the memorial of a denomination of Christians so well disposed to the public weal of their country." Backus was making headway, slowly but surely.

SEVEN

NEW LIBERTIES IN THE NEW WORLD

A LESSON IN CONTROLLING THE NARRATIVE

To obtain clear and just ideas of the affairs of the Baptists in New-England it seems necessary for us to look back to its first settlement, and carefully to examine what were the sentiments and character of the original planters.

Isaac Backus, *A History of New-England*

Controlling the narrative is a fundamental strategy of modern politics. It's the art of interpreting a tragedy or crisis or policy initiative or any sort of news by situating it within a broader context. It's telling people what an event *means* by identifying it as an episode in an ongoing story. *This is just another example of the systemic oppression of people of color. This is just another example of the liberal bias of the mainstream media. This is just another example . . .*

It's not a simple act of education. The goal is persuasion. The power to persuade doesn't lie in the facts themselves. The power lies in who can tell the most compelling story to *explain* the facts.

Controlling the narrative wasn't an invention of modern politics. Standing Order ministers who wanted to discredit Baptists spun the Baptists' efforts as an attack on Christian tradition. The movement was innovative—in a bad way. Isaac Backus was savvy enough to play the game, too. He responded with his own narrative—a massive three-volume narrative that took him nearly two decades to complete.

Controlling New England's Narrative

The Baptists' opponents wanted to discredit the Baptists as a fringe group with no historical pedigree, to paint them as innovators who had deviated from Christian tradition with their new perspectives on church membership and baptism. They wanted to demonstrate that these new interpretations had dangerous social implications, including creating division in the body of Christ. They went about this by telling two narratives.

The less frequently used narrative connected the American Baptists of the eighteenth century to a notorious group of European Anabaptists from the sixteenth century. In the early years of the Reformation in Germany, changes in the religious landscape led to real and violent trouble for many. The German Peasants' War of 1524–1525 was a widespread uprising of poor farmers who attempted to overthrow the ruling class. Their motivations were complex and multifaceted. But at some level they were emboldened by the rhetoric of Martin Luther. Luther defied the authority of popes and councils on the grounds that all humans are equals—at least *spiritual* equals—before God. Some of the rural poor interpreted the spirit of Luther's reformation as affirming a new social hierarchy that elevated the common person and brought the wealthy low. So they tried to bring the wealthy low with scythes and hoes. Luther denounced the peasants' rebellion in the strongest possible terms.

But they weren't the only group in Germany to see political possibilities in the theology of the Reformation. About a decade later, in January 1534, a group of German Anabaptists took control of the city of Münster. The term *Anabaptist* means "rebaptizer," and it referred to people who were baptized as adults. At the time, most citizens were baptized as infants in Roman Catholic Europe, so to be baptized as an adult meant to be baptized a second time. The rebels in Münster, who were derogatorily called the "madmen of Münster," forced many adults to be rebaptized. They destroyed religious icons and churches. They instituted polygamy in the city. They were terrifying. And the Standing Order sometimes accused the Baptists of New England of being the spiritual descendants of Münster's madmen. Painting New England's Baptists in this way was an attempt to highlight the danger of allowing the Baptist message to spread: these so-called Baptists *are just one more example of how straying from the church's teaching leads to violence and chaos.*

More often the Standing Order used a less sensational narrative to paint the Baptists as troublemaking newcomers. The narrative went like this: the founding fathers of New England, the Puritan settlers of Massachusetts, had established a good and godly society in the New World. That society was built on a firm foundation, a covenant between the founding fathers and God himself. That covenant was supported through infant baptism, which connected every child born in the colony to the promises of God. It was supported by an educated and rightly appointed minister whose salary was paid by local tax. This ensured qualified spiritual leadership in the colony that wasn't subject to changing opinion. For the covenant to work, everyone had to do their part. These Baptists threatened the whole experiment.

Backus countered this narrative with his own narrative. He included recent history throughout his writings with his accounts of persecution. At one point he responded to accusations that the Baptists of America were the spiritual descendants of Germany's violent rebaptizers. But the primary goal of his writings about history addressed the Standing Order's charge that somehow Baptists were compromising the faith of New England's founding fathers. He proposed a new narrative in which the Standing Order was the villain and the Baptists were the saviors of the founders' original vision.

Of course, to make that narrative work, he also had to redefine who the founders of New England were and what the original vision of New England was. Once the cast was assembled, Backus told a narrative of decline in which the Congregationalists and not the Baptists had deviated from New England tradition. He argued, furthermore, that as soon as the original vision of New England's founding fathers had been abandoned, persecution began creeping in and worsened until the present day. Backus's narrative was a tale of long, swift decline in which God raised up the Baptists to reverse the trend.

Defining "Founding Fathers": Pilgrims and Puritans

When the Standing Order used the phrase *founding fathers* of New England, they almost always referred to the men and women who settled the Massachusetts Bay Colony. Backus identified a different group as New England's founders: the Pilgrims.

According to Backus, the Pilgrims who colonized Plymouth in the 1620s set sail across a frigid ocean and scratched out a life in an unforgiving landscape because they were desperate to experience religious liberty. They had fled England first and found refuge in the Netherlands, a nation with a long history of tolerance for a wide range of dissidents. From there they headed to the New World with hopes of establishing a society in which they could live and worship freely without fear of persecution. The prospect of being English colonists gave them a chance to reconnect with the Motherland without subjecting themselves to persecution at home. The England they left was not merely resistant to their *ideas*; it also banned public meetings and corporate worship. In short, in Backus's view, the Plymouth

Pilgrims were not simply idealists in search of mental space to try out a new idea. They were religious refugees in search of sanctuary.

According to Backus, the Plymouth colonists held a couple of convictions that got them into trouble with England's dominant religious classes. First, they rejected infant baptism. They believed a person should be immersed as a sign of their personal faith in Jesus. An infant can't have—or certainly can't *demonstrate*—personal faith in Jesus. So only adult believers should be baptized.

This conviction amounted to a rejection of a centuries-old practice in England. But that was not all. The Plymouth settlers also rejected the idea that the civil government ought to regulate religious rules. They believed God had instituted government for peoples' good, but that its job was limited to enforcing public safety. Church and state, ecclesiastical and civil powers, operated in separate spheres and had different responsibilities, though both were ordained by God. This was a radical idea in the eighteenth century, and these refugees were ready to experiment by putting these ideas into practice. For a generation or so, Backus claimed, Plymouth was the model colony of religious liberty. Dissenters of various sorts enjoyed liberties in Plymouth that they wouldn't have found elsewhere. Quakers and others were free to think, and gather, practice as they believed God expected them to and felt bound by their conscience to do so.

Enter the villain.

The Puritans who founded the Massachusetts Bay Colony arrived in the New World just a decade after the Pilgrims. Some Puritans took up arms in a bloody conflict in England to try to make England the place they were free to be Puritan. When that didn't work, some struck out for the New World to try a different experiment. In 1630, they journeyed to America with the goal of finding freedom to worship. While they disagreed with the Church of England on a number of theological issues, they retained the two commitments the folks in Plymouth rejected. They maintained a commitment to infant baptism because they believed it was God's way of passing his promises to his people. And they maintained the idea that church and state should work together to ensure proper worship and Christian behavior.

The Puritan vision of liberty in the New World was not a vision for radical freedom for all but a vision for freedom to be Puritan and implement a Puritan vision of society. In other words, the Pilgrims of Plymouth and the Puritans of Massachusetts both cherished "religious liberty" dearly. It was, as one pastor said, "a darling point" among them. Even so the two groups meant something very different when they used the phrase *religious liberty*. Unfortunately for the colonists who were not Puritan, Massachusetts won influence early on and exerted a disproportionate sway on other New England colonies.

This was not by accident. Governor John Winthrop of Massachusetts expected his colony to be an example to the world. It was their destiny to model how to live as a society submitted to

God's will. If they are successful, Winthrop told his people, "He shall make us a praise and glory that men shall say of succeeding plantations, 'may the Lord make it like of that New England.'" For Winthrop, the settlers of Massachusetts should gladly accept their role as an example to the nations: "For we must consider that we shall be as a city upon a hill. The eyes of all people are upon us. So that if we shall deal falsely with our God in this work we have undertaken, and so cause Him to withdraw His present help from us, we shall be made a story and a by-word through the world." The expectation that "the eyes of the world" were upon them was grandiose. It turned out to be true.

Massachusetts was successful in part because it was well organized. Locals were required to submit the names of the newly born, newly deceased, or newly married members of their families, and include the payment of a penny to cover the cost of record keeping. Church records were kept equally carefully—records of active members and sinners on probation. The colony's propensity for record keeping made an important piece of legislation easy to institute.

In an effort to ensure civil stability, the General Court in Boston required candidates for political office to be members of approved religious institutions. The rule would be easy to enforce, since the colony kept a careful record of church attendance. Nevertheless this legislation moved beyond record keeping and was aimed at regulation. Individuals were considered fit for office only if they attended an approved congregation, and the options were limited. Catholics, Quakers, Baptists, and others need not apply.

The year was 1631. As Backus told the story, it was the beginning of the end of religious liberty in America.

Boston eventually gave its civil government authority to punish citizens who broke religious regulations. Sinners could be excommunicated from their churches for, say, breaking the sabbath. If they remained unrepentant for six months, jurisdiction passed from clergy to constable. In addition to spiritual consequences, the lapsed were subject to civil punishment in the form of fines and jail time. Quakers were banished from the colony altogether. If Quakers returned to the colony after being banished, they could have one of their ears cut off. If they came back again, they lost the other ear. Quakers were targeted first, but they were not the only ones. Anyone who openly condemned baptizing infants, including parents who refused to have their own infants baptized, were subject to both excommunication from the church and exile from the colony.

These changes were gradually and inevitably adopted by surrounding colonies. The personalities in charge in colonial Massachusetts were so forceful and bold that they eventually exerted influence throughout all New England. One citizen of Plymouth observed this influence by admitting that the "Plymouth saddle is on the Bay horse." Where Massachusetts goes, so go the neighbors.

A Faithful Remnant

The rise of the Puritan view of faith and life may have dominated the legislation of America's New England colonies, but Backus argued it didn't squash the spirit of radical liberty in New England's citizens. Nor did it eliminate their vision of a society guided by a clear separation of church and state. As Massachusetts moved to standardize and homogenize its religious and social life, citizens with a different vision for society founded new colonies.

Roger Williams, for example, arrived in the American colonies from England in 1631, the same year as the Boston General Court ruling that required magistrates to be members of approved congregations. At first Williams was accepted as a man "of good account in England for a godly preacher." But he lost favor soon enough with local powers. Williams's story is complex and interesting, but the short version goes like this: he refused to join the established church in Boston and refused to acknowledge that the civil rulers had authority to punish religious beliefs. Williams went to Plymouth for a while, where he was welcomed. But within a year or so, Mr. Cotton of Boston banished him from the colony of Massachusetts—on account of his religious convictions. Williams went on to found Rhode Island, a colony that practiced radical religious liberty.

Thus Roger Williams became America's first and most famous exile for religious liberty. He spent the remainder of his life writing from exile to advocate for religious tolerance.

Others soon felt the tightening grip of Puritan authority in Massachusetts. Some, like Williams and Anne Hutchinson, were banished. Others left willingly to plant new colonies, leading to a flurry of foundings in the 1600s. Connecticut was established by citizens of Massachusetts who chafed under the new collusion of church and state there. Later, when certain towns in Connecticut appeared ready to hitch their wagons to the "Bay horse," people started even more new towns.

The way Backus told the story, the emergence of new colonies testifies to a trend toward greater restriction and less liberty. Those colonies were founded because people *longed* for liberty but were not experiencing it in New England. Connecticut and Rhode Island were both founded by citizens of Massachusetts who felt their liberties curtailed by oppressive developments in church and city government. The reason people had to keep fighting for freedom was because freedom kept slipping away.

Another way to say all this is that Backus believed the "founding vision for the New World" lasted only nine years; then a new vision cut in on the Plymouth brethren. These two visions had two competing ideas of religious liberty. The first, represented by Plymouth, believed religious liberty meant all people were protected to hold whatever religious views they had without fear of punishment from the civil court. The second, represented by Boston, believed religious liberty meant the freedom to believe according to their particular interpretation of Christian Scripture and theology.

According to Backus, the founders of Rhode Island and Connecticut had to keep moving, keep exploring, keep building to preserve liberties. The dream of liberty, the vision of the founders of Massachusetts, was always *that close* to extinction. Backus and his kin weren't fighting for *new* liberties. They were fighting to preserve the old ones. And by the time Backus was born, the Puritan vision of liberty was gaining traction and edging out the founding vision of America.

Far from being purely objective, this narrative was deeply personal for Backus. His own genealogy is woven through this tale. The colony of Connecticut, in which Backus was born, was founded by a hundred residents of the Massachusetts Bay Colony who struck out to form a new social experiment. Isaac grew up in a territory that self-consciously cast off the way Massachusetts did things.

By 1660, another split over religious values brought the Backus family more directly into this story. The church in the village of Saybrook, Connecticut, started adopting practices that some members disapproved of. For example, instead of ordaining ministers simply by laying hands on them, the Saybrook church began to include a council of ministers and churches from the area. This was a first step down the slope to Presbyterianism, in the minds of many. More to the point, the new policy took authority away from members of the congregation and put it in the hands of outsiders. It meant that a council of ministers from other towns chose the local minister. Many in Saybrook considered this a violation of religious liberty.

So, in 1660, Pastor James Fitch led a majority of his congregants not only to start a new church but indeed to plant a new town called Norwich. The settlers of Norwich were motivated to start a new settlement primarily for religious reasons, to live according to their religious values. Among those who left Saybrook to found Norwich was Isaac Backus's great-grandfather.

Backus's first biographer, Alvah Hovey, considered all this information essential for understanding what motivated the Baptist pastor and shaped his vision and values. I think he's right. "It will be found that his course in manhood was in no small degree the result of his training in boyhood," Hovey wrote, "that his character through life was the ever ripening fruit of seed planted in his mind when a child. From the atmosphere of piety and freedom which pervaded the home of his youth he inhaled the spirit which animated him to the hour of death."

It didn't take long for the Puritans to start talking about themselves as the "founding fathers" of New England and their vision as the continent's original vision. Backus wouldn't have it: the Pilgrims were the true founding fathers of the New World. *Their* vision for radical religious liberty came first, he insisted. *Their* vision inspired the founding of new colonies, including his home colony of Connecticut. The Puritans cut in later and imposed a foreign vision. Throughout his life, the Standing Order—Congregationalists whose ministers were financed by a tax on the general public—would accuse Backus and his fellow Baptists of breaking with tradition and therefore threatening the Christian experiment with their "innovative" ideas about baptism and liberty of conscience. Backus consistently argued that he wasn't inventing or innovating anything. As he saw it, the Baptists had recovered the original vision of America's true founding fathers, the Plymouth Pilgrims, which had been lost to history and regained by the Baptists.

Blinded by the Battle

The danger of trying to control the narrative is that it's entirely possible to be boxed in by your own narrative. Backus mined history for a defense against one main objection—that he and the Baptists were theological and social innovators—and to point out how far New England had fallen from its former glory. He got a lot of things right. The problem with Backus's approach is that he conceded the point that the original vision of the founding fathers of New England was at some level *the* deciding factor in the debate. He defined *founding fathers* differently than his enemies did. But he more or less adopted the opposing narrative and tried to swap out the characters.

There is a real risk when we try to control the narrative that we will argue from the wrong narrative. Two narratives create problems for many advocates for religious liberty today. First is the narrative that America has *always* been a Christian nation, founded on Christian values, and that the nation has been experiencing a steady decline away from our founding principles of faith. The other narrative is that America has always been committed to religious liberty (although not a

Christian nation), and that in recent years that commitment to liberty is increasingly violated.

The problem with these narratives is that they are easily falsifiable. It is easy to identify "founding fathers" of the Revolutionary period—signers of the Declaration of Independence, framers of the Constitution, early presidents—who were not men of faith and who were self-consciously committed to founding America on *secular* principles, not Christian ones. And whether or not Backus was right about church history in America, his collected stories of persecution challenge the claim that America has always valued religious liberty.

Backus's narrative could have been more successful if he had taken it back further. He was conscious of swimming in the stream of the Reformation, but he didn't take his history all the way back to the Reformation. If he had, he would have found a more robust argument. The Reformation heritage offers great resources for civil liberties, including religious liberty. He could have brought the full weight of the tradition to bear on the issue. Not just since Plymouth but since John Calvin's Geneva, the Protestant tradition has been on a trajectory to extend civil and religious liberties.

A number of scholars, beginning with Barry Alan Shain, have developed a convincing case that the heritage of religious liberty in America is actually attributable not to secular philosophers like John Locke but to the Reformed tradition in America. Among the most forceful advocates of this thesis are legal historians, including Peter Judson Richards and John Witte Jr.

Witte's expansive project is advancing "a new history of Western rights" in which he argues that "Calvin and his followers developed a distinct theology and jurisprudence of human rights and gradually cast these into enduring institutional and constitutional forms in early modern Europe and America." Witte's work challenges the popularly held assumption that laws securing religious liberty were a modern Enlightenment victory over religion itself. A growing number of historians are recognizing that, in America at least, disestablishment "was a populist movement where religious, and not Enlightenment, influences predominated."

Locating a commitment to liberty in the Christian tradition instead of the American tradition should strengthen our resolve to protect religious freedom. We protect religious liberty not because the right is enshrined in our founding documents but because of our conviction that faith can't be inherited or imposed. It has to be embraced voluntarily. We advocate for the legal protection of religious liberty because as fallen human beings we know we are prone to exploit the weak in our own self-interest. Neither of these statements requires America to have been a Christian nation or committed to religious liberty from the beginning.

To me, this seems like a helpful way forward. Debates quickly become derailed by arguments about whose political position best reflects the perspectives of the founding fathers. We should probably arrive at the point where appeal to founding fathers is part of the argument but not the extent of it. I look forward to the day people say of Christians, *This is just one more example of the Christian commitment to religious liberty.*

It took Backus almost twenty years to complete his *History of New-England*. In those years he continued to advocate for religious liberty. But he turned his focus back to local matters, especially the growth and health of the Baptist movement. While the first half of his ministry was marked by extraordinary productivity, the last decades were marked by extraordinary influence. That influence included finally securing the religious liberty he struggled for all his adult life.

EIGHT

BACKUS, BAPTISTS, AND THE BILL OF RIGHTS

Every person has an unalienable right to act in all religious affairs according to the full persuasion of his own mind.

Isaac Backus, Proposed Bill of Rights

After the Continental Congress in 1774, Backus took his fight for freedom back to the local level. Because the Congress was limited in scope to federal issues, and because it considered religious liberty a local issue, the debates took place there. Dissenters successfully secured religious liberty in other states long before religious establishment finally ended in Massachusetts. And in other states, including Virginia, Baptists led the charge for soul liberty.

In the years immediately following America's declaration of independence from England, each of the states began drafting constitutions. Efforts to formalize a constitution for Massachusetts gave Isaac Backus the opportunity to speak up for the rights of Baptists in the region. A proposed constitution in 1777 included a provision to reinstate religious taxes on all citizens. That draft of the constitution failed to pass for a number of reasons. But the issue of religious taxation didn't go away. It was the subject of much writing and debating for nearly the remainder of the eighteenth century.

In 1779, a delegation met in Cambridge, Massachusetts, to discuss and adopt a state constitution. A proposed draft gave the state authority to tax citizens in order to raise "suitable provision" for ministers. This created considerable debate. Those who objected to state interference in religious matters quoted Backus's history of abuses in New England to show the dangers of giving the state the power to punish religious offenders. Those in favor of the proposal apparently included John Adams and Robert Treat Paine, who had heard Backus's presentation at the Continental Congress in 1774. They argued that a state-supported church ensured the public order and provided social unity and stability. In the end, the "obnoxious principle" of state taxation was preserved in the draft, which passed by a majority vote. This was a considerable blow to Baptist interests. At this point they had been struggling for more than forty years to break free from religious taxation and the presumptive authority it represented. Now this authority was updated and codified in the state's official documents.

The vote was even more personal for Backus. For one, Backus had drafted a proposed bill of rights protecting religious liberty, which he submitted to the committee for consideration. It is reproduced here in its entirety. Note the similarities between the language Backus proposed and the language that was ultimately adopted in the Bill of Rights:

1. All men are born equally free and independent, and have certain natural, inherent and unalienable rights, among which are enjoying and defending life and liberty, acquiring, possessing, and protecting property, and pursuing and obtaining happiness and safety.
2. As God is the only worthy object of all religious worship, and nothing can be true religion but a voluntary obedience unto his revealed will, of which each rational soul has an equal right to judge for itself; every person has an unalienable right to act in all religious affairs according to the full persuasion of his own mind, where others are not injured thereby. And civil rulers are so far from having any right to empower any person or persons, to judge for others in such affairs, and to enforce their judgments with the sword, that their power ought to be exerted to protect all persons and societies, within their jurisdiction from being injured or interrupted in the free enjoyment of this right, under any pretense whatsoever.
3. The people of this state have the sole, exclusive, and inherent right of governing and regulating the internal police of the same.
4. As all civil rulers derive their authority from the people, so they are accountable to them for the use they make of it.

5. The great end of government being for the good of the governed, and not the honor or profit of any particular persons or families therein; the community hath an unalienable right to reform, alter, or newly form their constitution or government, as that community shall judge to be most conducive to the public weal.
6. It being essential to civil freedom that every elector of officers should give his vote with an unbiased mind; whoever shall make use of any sort of bribery, or party influence, either to get into office or to keep himself in place thereby seeks to rob the freemen of their birthright, and ought to be look upon as an enemy to liberty, and not to be trusted with any public office. Elections ought to be free and frequent.
7. Every member of civil society hath a right to be protected in the enjoyment of life, liberty and property, and therefore is bound to contribute his portion towards the expenses of that protection, and to yield his personal services, when necessary, or an equivalent thereto: but no part of any man's property can justly be taken from him, or applied to public uses, without his own consent, or that of his legal representatives: and no man ought to be compelled to bear arms, who conscientiously scruples the lawfulness of it, if he will pay such equivalent; nor are the people bound by any laws, but such as they have in like manner assented to, for their common good.

8. In all prosecutions for criminal offences, a man hath a right to be heard by himself and his council, to demand the cause and nature of his accusations, to be confronted with the witnesses, to call for evidence in his favor, and a speedy public trial, by an impartial jury of the country, without whose consent he cannot be found guilty. Nor can he be compelled to give evidence against himself: nor can any man be justly deprived of his liberty, except by the laws of the land, or the judgment of his peers.
9. The people have a right to hold themselves, their houses, papers and possessions free from search or seizure; therefore warrants without oaths or affirmations first made, affording a sufficient foundation for them, and whereby an officer or messenger may be required to search suspected places, or seize any person or persons, his or their property, not particularly described, are contrary to that right, and ought not to be granted.
10. In all controversies respecting property, and in suits between man and man, the parties have a right to trial by jury, which ought to be held sacred.
11. The people have a right to freedom of speech, and of writing and publishing their sentiments; therefore the freedom of the press ought not to be restrained.
12. The people have a right to bear arms for the defense of themselves and the state; and as standing armies, in time of peace, are dangerous to liberty, they ought not to be

kept up; and the military should be kept under strict subordination to, and governed by, the civil power.

13. A frequent recurrence to the first principles of government, and a firm adherence to justice, moderation, temperance, industry, and frugality, are absolutely necessary to preserve the great blessings of government and liberty; and the people have a right to assemble together, to consult about these great concerns, to instruct their representatives, and to apply to the legislature for a redress of grievances, by address, petition, or remonstrance.

Backus's hard work in developing this bill of rights seemed futile when it was rejected by the committee assembled in 1779. Worse for Backus, though, is that the politicians who led the vote to ratify the new doctrine swayed some to vote in favor of it by claiming that the list of grievances Backus had presented in his earlier writings, including the argument he made before the delegates for the Continental Congress, was either exaggerated or altogether fabricated.

"I am informed by several members of the convention . . . that to obtain the above described power over us," Backus wrote in his printed response, "Mr. John Adams and Mr. Paine brought up the above named accusation against us, and that Mr. Paine said he had reason to think that some things, mentioned in our memorial, never existed." They argued the Baptists had sent Backus to Philadelphia in 1774 with "a false memorial of grievances, in order to break the union of these colonies." Backus didn't take the accusation lying down. He wrote a tract to publicize the accusation and denounce it. His tract "Independent Chronicle" expresses his frustration with the committee and his confidence in his previous work:

> This is therefore to give notice that I am ready to meet them before any proper judges, when called, to answer for every word therein, and to suffer deserved punishment if I am convicted of advancing any one accusation against my country, or against any person therein, that I cannot support.

Backus was prepared to fight publicly and permanently these men, Paine and Adams, who today enjoy reputations as true defenders of liberty. If "those gentlemen should persist in their accusations against us without fairly supporting them," Backus warned, "the public will judge how far they will deserve regard for the future."

Backus was right to fear the consequences of the new constitution. Two members of the convention who lived in Bridgewater felt emboldened by the accusations Adams and Paine made at the convention. When these delegates returned home, they sent a tax collector and constable to arrest two members of the First Baptist Church in Middleboro for failing to pay their ecclesiastical taxes. When the brothers objected to the arrest, the constable argued, "Our churches are built upon the law."

"I knew that before," one of the brothers replied, "but I thought you would be ashamed to own it."

The First Amendment to the United States Constitution

While the most vigorous efforts for liberty took place at the state level, discussions about religious liberty continued at the national level. In 1787, a Constitutional Convention proposed a new constitution. A delegate to the convention from Virginia proposed a bill of rights that clarified and secured civil liberties. It seems safe to assume that everyone present supported the idea of a bill of rights for the constitution. They didn't. Some opposed including a bill of rights because they believed the language of the proposed constitution was enough to secure civil liberties. As James Madison put it, there was no reason to guarantee religious liberty in a bill of rights, because "there is not a shadow of right in the general government to intermeddle with religion." There's no need to clarify; everyone *knows* the government has no right to meddle in religious affairs.

Others feared more fundamentally that listing specific liberties at all was dangerous because it risked communicating that the only rights protected are the ones that are listed. Could any committee possibly generate a comprehensive list? "A bill of rights is neither an essential nor a necessary instrument in framing a system of government, since liberty may exist and be as well secured without it," argued James Wilson. He continued,

> But it was not only unnecessary, but on this occasion it was found impracticable—for who will be bold enough to undertake to enumerate all the rights of the people?—and when the attempt to enumerate them is made, it must be

> remembered that if the enumeration is not complete, everything not expressly mentioned will be presumed to be purposely omitted.

This negative view of a bill of rights prevailed at the convention of 1787, and the delegates voted unanimously to proceed with the new constitution without amendments.

Logistically the delay created problems. In order to be ratified, the new federal constitution had to be approved by nine of the thirteen original American states. Several states, including Virginia and Massachusetts, were not inclined to ratify the constitution without a bill of rights protecting civil liberties. Baptists in these regions, especially, feared centralizing power in the federal government. For them, a stronger national government was analogous to centralized Presbyterian or Anglican Church polity. They believed in the autonomy of the local congregation and that belief translated into distaste for centralized federal power.

It was Baptists in Virginia, in fact, who fought most successfully to include a provision to protect religious liberty. In 1775, John Leland began his fourteen-year tenure of itinerant preaching and political activity in Virginia, fighting tooth and nail for the separation of church and state. When Virginia was considering ratifying the federal constitution, Leland ran against James Madison as Orange County representative to the Virginia convention. Leland and the Baptists opposed ratification because it made no provision for religious liberty;

Madison favored ratification without specific language protecting religious freedom.

Fearing that Leland would win the election in the heavily Baptist county, Madison met with Leland in Leland's home prior to the election and discussed the issue at length. Subsequently, Leland withdrew from the race, Madison was elected, and Virginia voted in favor of ratification. Joseph Dawson argues that while most modern Americans hold Madison most responsible for the Constitutional guarantee of religious freedom, Madison, if asked, would likely give credit to John Leland. Leland made it his life's work to fight against the Anglican establishment in Virginia and, upon returning to New England in 1791, against the Congregational establishment in Massachusetts and Connecticut. He was active in framing Connecticut's state constitution.

A convention of Massachusetts delegates met in 1788 to debate ratifying the new US Constitution. Backus was nominated by the citizens of Middleborough as one of four delegates from the town. This was the only political office Backus ever held. His selection speaks to his influence in the region and the esteem with which he was held among his peers. His Baptist peers had chosen the delegates to represent their case in front of national figures through the Grievance Committee. Now his neighbors, Baptists and non-Baptists alike, entrusted him with the task of debating the new Constitution.

After listening to other delegates express their perspectives on the Constitution, Backus became convinced that ratification was the right decision. Once his mind was made up, he became the first Baptist delegate at the convention to argue in favor of it. He made a speech before the delegates in which he praised the wording of the Constitution for "excluding all titles of nobility, or hereditary succession of power," for, he said, "the American revolution was built upon the principle, that all men are born with an equal right to liberty and property." There was room for improvement, Backus admitted, but he recognized that "a door is now opened, for the establishment of righteous government, and for securing equal liberty, as never was before opened to any people on earth."

The opportunities for equal liberty that lay before America included the end of slavery in the new nation, and Backus took a moment in his speech to advocate for abolition. "No man abhors that wicked practice more than I do," he said, and "a door is now open" to "hinder the importation of slaves into any of these states." Even so, Backus reflected the blindness of his age to the extent that he didn't think abolition needed to be written into the Constitution. Instead, "each state is at liberty now to abolish slavery as soon as they please." This was the first time in all of Backus's writings that he mentioned the institution of slavery directly. The irony is palpable from this side of history. Backus considered religious liberty a federal issue and slavery a state issue.

Ultimately, the Constitution was ratified in 1791, and the accepted version included the Bill of Rights as we know it today. The First Amendment protects the free exercise of religion. The problem was the Bill of Rights only protected religious liberty at the *federal* level. It had no jurisdiction to enforce religious liberty at the state level. It said, "*Congress* shall make no law respecting an establishment of religion," but it left state legislatures free to make and enforce such laws. Baptists in Massachusetts continued to strain under limits of liberty.

Stirrings of Another Awakening

Some Baptists in Massachusetts began to lose heart when it appeared ongoing religious taxation was inevitable. Backus was either more optimistic or more stubborn. He undertook a preaching tour of the Southern colonies of Virginia and North Carolina, where he was surprised—and pleased—to discover that many of the leading Baptists in those states were also leading men in society. There was no stigma attached to being Baptist in the South, as there was in New England. Seeing the status of Baptists in the South renewed his hope for the Baptists' future in New England. The trip was long and demanding, but it lifted his spirits. "Between January 10 and May 27," Backus wrote in his journal, "I travelled in North-Carolina and Virginia 1251 miles, and preached 117 sermons, generally to people who were very earnest to hear the word." What impressed Backus most is not what he himself accomplished but what he considered to be the work of God in the region:

> The church of England, which was supported by law till the late war, is now fallen into contempt, and the law to support their ministers by tax has been repealed above

> 3 years; and the Baptists are in the best credit with their rulers of any denomination in Virginia, as well as North-Carolina. O, what hath God wrought!

Backus summarized his tour of the South simply: "The greatest journey I ever went."

Backus didn't give up the fight for liberty after 1788. In 1790 he sent a letter to then president George Washington and included in the package the first two volumes (the final volume was not yet complete) of his *History of New-England*, Backus's revisionist history about liberty in the New World. Backus was humble about the book. "Indeed, if elegance of style and composition were necessary to render any book acceptable to your Excellency, the author would not have presumed to send you such a present as his History of New England." He sent it just the same because he believed it contained "the knowledge of principles and facts, and of their influence on mankind through various changes" that were of great importance to the president.

Despite these continued efforts in support of religious liberty, Backus focused more on ministry and less on politics in the last decade of his life. "From 1790 to 1797 he annually rode over 1,100 miles on horseback throughout New England, delivering an average of 150 sermons each year and participating in numerous councils."

The rigorous preaching schedule Backus maintained was motivated in large part by the growing sense he had that America was due for another revival. The number of Baptists was growing, and this was a good thing. Gradually, Baptists established a reputation for respectability, leaving behind its stigma of aberrance, and this was a good thing too. But Backus believed these gains came at a cost. The piety of the movement had begun to cool, he felt. He traveled and preached, in part, to help foster the sort of revival among his Baptist brothers and sisters that began his journey of faith a half century before.

One way Baptists worked to bring revival was through the Massachusetts Baptists' first missionary fund, begun in 1798, which primarily financed the planting of Baptist churches in the frontier regions of New England. The Massachusetts Baptist Missionary Society began foreign mission work and launched a magazine in 1803. Backus was a charter subscriber to the publication, the *Massachusetts Missionary Magazine*, which was the first Baptist periodical in America. Backus managed to open the annual meeting in prayer in 1804, despite his failing health.

Backus's health began to decline rapidly after 1798. He suffered from what appears to have been prostate cancer or at least prostate inflammation—perhaps aggravated by the thousands of miles he logged itinerating on horseback. He tried several rounds of home cures and other treatments, including ingesting liquid mercury. In 1788, he had traveled more than 1,200 miles and preached more than one hundred sermons. A decade later, in 1798, he traveled only twenty miles and managed to deliver only twenty sermons.

More devastating to Backus than his own declining health was his wife's illness. In the autumn months of 1800, Susanna endured a period of several weeks during which she scarcely ate and experienced serious internal pain. Backus noted that she "bore it with great patience, and never experienced any fears of death." On November 12 a church member visited the Backus home to pray for Susanna. The visitor asked Susanna how he could pray for her. She replied, "I am not so much concerned about living or dying, as to have my will swallowed up in the will of God." For nearly two weeks she "wasted away" until the early morning hours of November 24, when "she expired without any great struggles." Susanna was buried on November 26. Backus preached the annual Thanksgiving service on November 27.

Backus summarized the year briefly in his journal entry for December 31, 1800: "In the year past I have had many disorders, and have travelled abroad but 121 miles, yet have preached 113 times. The change in my family is unspeakably great, yet my mind has been upheld by God beyond expectation."

It became something of a pastime of Backus's old age to log the deaths of friends and church members in his diary. In 1801 he "noted sadly that only fourteen persons were still alive among the sixty-one who had joined the Separate Church in Middleborough during the first ten months it was founding in 1747/48, and only five of these were still living in the town and attending his church."

Declining health kept Backus from preaching for weeks at a time, even in his own church. But he was encouraged by signs that the revival he had been praying and striving for was finally happening. Year after year, grief and illness were eclipsed by news of what Backus considered the work of God in America. "Although stupidity has greatly prevailed in our land," Backus wrote on New Year's Eve, 1801, "yet religion has been revived in many places." One sign of revival was the growth of Baptist numbers throughout America. Backus quotes a letter from a Baptist minister from Georgia:

> According to the best accounts from Kentucky, there has been added to the Baptist churches since last March near 6,000. . . . There are six Baptist associations in that state. Of these the Elkhorn is perhaps the smallest, and from their minutes last August it appears that their number is 3,011 souls.

By 1803, Backus lacked the strength to travel the short distance from home to the church building. His congregation loved and admired him deeply, and when he was absent a young man named Ezra Kendall filled the pulpit. In 1804 the church voted that it was time for Backus to retire and for Kendall to replace him as pastor. Backus supported the decision. Under Kendall's spiritual care, the congregation showed signs of revival. "Thirteen persons were converted in the fall of 1804 and ten more by August of 1805." In September, Backus met with a group from the Warren Association in the town "where it first began in

1767." The meeting boasted "the largest number of ministers . . . and it was as agreeable [a] meeting as I ever had with them in 35 times." These were the early years of a movement historians would later call the Second Great Awakening.

In March of 1806, Backus suffered a stroke. One arm still paralyzed, he mustered his strength and preached his last sermon on April 3. He suffered a second stroke on April 20 and died on November 20.

Massachusetts still supported Congregational ministers with ecclesiastical taxes until 1833, almost thirty years after Backus died. Nevertheless he lived long enough to see the first fruits of his lifetime of labor for religious liberty. The testimony of one of his neighbors, a Congregational minister—a man who represented Backus's chief opposition for his entire adult life—illustrates the influence and reputation Backus enjoyed at the end of his life.

> Mr. Backus was called "Father" not only by his own people, who might well thus honor him, but by almost the entire community; and a Patriarch he was, not only by ecclesiastical powers, but as a Pastor and Divine, and in moral power and weight of well-earned and well-established character.

More than two hundred years later, Backus's influence can still be felt in the America he helped shape. One Backus biographer noted that Backus was not the most articulate or influential man of his generation. "Greater men than he expressed the theological, the political, the Enlightenment views of the latter part of the eighteenth century—Edwards, Jefferson, Franklin." What makes Backus compelling, though, is not his intellect. Backus's appeal "lies in his almost perfect embodiment of the evangelical spirit of his times." His example has much to offer the evangelical spirit of our own times.

NINE

WHERE TO GO FROM HERE

This story will elicit a range of responses.

Some readers will be disappointed this book was not more comprehensive. Isaac Backus strove for more than half a century to secure legal protection for his fellow Baptists in New England and throughout the new United States. This struggle took place in a broader context and included a cast of characters barely alluded to in this volume. Readers wanting a deeper immersion into the period and its complicated issues are right to be disappointed. As a consolation, I've included a short few paragraphs below that offer suggested additional reading about Isaac Backus, evangelical engagement with the broader culture, and the Reformed and evangelical contributions to Western ideas about religious liberty.

Alternatively, it's possible for many other readers that this story has introduced a range of new and potentially challenging ideas. Much of what drove the formulation of the First Amendment, for example, were the experiences of marginalized religious groups in the American colonies. In the popular imagination, and according to the way we often hear the story of religious liberty in schools and the media and other public outlets, we often talk about the legal protection of religious liberty as if it were already in place when European settlers started colonizing the New World. They came here, we imply, because that legal protection was already in place. It would be more accurate to say they came here for the potential, the possibility, of weaving religious liberty into the American fabric. In actual fact, religious liberty is an aspiration we have not yet fully and completely achieved. Moreover, the legislation that now protects religious practice in America is in place to protect ourselves against our own tendency to marginalize groups we find threatening.

Reading between the lines, we see other challenging realities, including the work of state legislatures to consolidate religious authority in the hands of privileged Christian denominations (and the identity of the privileged denomination changed from state to state). The early federal government was at best agnostic about and at worst complicit in ongoing religious establishments until well into the nineteenth century.

It's worth asking: If we missed this, what else have we missed? There's a strong analogy in my mind between the nation's track record on religious liberty and our track record on civil rights. That "all men are created equal" and that there should be "liberty and justice for all" are, like religious liberty, aspirational values in American culture we have always been reaching toward but have never fully attained. In the last half century both state and federal legislatures have actively worked against civil liberties in an effort to privilege the rights of the white majority over the rights of ethnic minorities. A key difference between religious liberties and civil liberties in America is that we have come much further much faster in securing religious liberty for people of all creeds.

The reason I bring this up is because at this historical moment, the last years of the first quarter of the twenty-first century, Christians in America are facing serious issues we were able to avoid just a couple of decades ago. Increasingly the value and sincerity of our faith is tested on the basis of how we respond to needs and answer questions about sexuality and gender, liberty and equality, race and ethnicity. How we move forward over this difficult terrain will be determined, at least in part, by how well we understand our history, how willing we are to confess our past sins, how able we are to learn from our mistakes.

How we move forward will also be determined, at least in part, by how we perceive our roles in this drama. Do we imagine ourselves to be the marginalized victim whose liberties are increasingly infringed? Or do we imagine ourselves to be the established elite, whose power continues to subjugate men and women with different values and lifestyles?

Not long ago I heard an organizer of a large event say to hundreds of attendees, "It is crucial that our stories are heard in mainstream media, so that people who have experienced the things we have experienced don't feel isolated and alone. It is crucial that our community and our values are accurately represented in the media, where they are often misrepresented. This has never been more important than it is today, when our values are so blatantly under attack." These words easily could have been spoken at any gathering of political conservatives or evangelical Christians. Instead, they were spoken by the lesbian organizer of an LGBT film festival. So many groups in American public life view themselves as the underdog. Whether we view ourselves as in power or on the margins will have a huge influence on how we imagine our contribution to ongoing discussions about liberty of all sorts in an increasingly diverse America, including religious liberty.

Isaac Backus certainly would be delighted to know that his work was being used to prompt discussion about how to live faithfully in a complicated world. In his own day, he hoped his writing would help his compatriots "to avoid evil ways; especially to guard against all cruelty, deceit, and violence." It would be a great honor to his memory if, more than two hundred years after his death, his work continued to help us better understand the past that we may envision a more equitable future.

More About Isaac Backus

If it accomplishes nothing else, perhaps this book will inspire you to learn more about Isaac Backus.

There are essentially three biographies of Backus in publication. One of them, *Isaac Backus: Pioneer Champion of Religious Liberty* by T. B. Maston, can be hard to find. Perhaps for this reason, it is not frequently cited in research about Backus. The other two biographies have been more influential.

The first was published in 1859, more than fifty years after Backus's death. Alvah Hovey's *A Memoir of the Life and Times of the Rev. Isaac Backus, A. M.* treats Backus in glowing terms. It is sound history, but the tone verges on hagiography in places. The narrative emphasizes Backus's efforts for religious liberty and draws heavily on primary sources.

The second, *Isaac Backus and the American Pietist Tradition* by William G. McLoughlin, is the most recent biography of Backus. It was published in 1967. The book is short and engaging, and McLoughlin was an expert in both the era and in the history of Baptists in America. In my opinion, though, he misunderstands Backus in a couple of important ways. The primary problem is that McLoughlin doesn't take Backus's theology seriously enough. The truth about Backus is probably somewhere between Hovey's and McLoughlin's treatments of him.

The best way to get to know Backus is in his own words. McLoughlin released a volume of collected works by Backus called *Isaac Backus on Church, State, and Calvinism: Pamphlets, 1754–1789*. See also the complete list of works by Backus in the appendix.

Evangelical Engagement with American Culture

I started thinking differently about religious liberty when the narrative that America had always been a thoroughly Christian nation began to wear thin. Consider becoming better acquainted with the general landscape of religious life in early America. George Marsden's classic text *Religion and American Life* demonstrates that America is always becoming *both* more religious *and* more secular at the same time—and always has been. This narrative provides an interesting lens through which to view the issue of religious liberty.

D. Michael Lindsay's book *Faith in the Halls of Power* tells the story of how once-marginalized evangelicals rose to positions of influence in American politics and popular culture. It is an interesting in-their-own-words approach based on hundreds of interviews with evangelical leaders. If Lindsay's book touches on the consolidation of evangelical power, Kenneth Collins covers similar ground but emphasizes *Power, Politics and the Fragmentation of Evangelicalism* as his title suggests.

Together these volumes help to articulate what evangelicals have aspired to in terms of cultural influence, and what many evangelicals consider at stake in ongoing debates about religious liberty.

Evangelical Origins of Religious Liberty

Perhaps the most intellectually stimulating topic raised in this study is the evangelical Protestant contribution to civil (including religious) liberties in Western culture. There is a large and growing body of work on this topic. These sources will be a good place to start.

John Witte Jr. has produced several volumes on the interrelated subjects of religious liberty, theology, legislation, and history. *The Reformation of Rights* explores the contributions of Calvinist Protestants to the development of human rights from sixteenth-century Geneva, Switzerland, to eighteenth-century America. Witte's *Religion and the American Constitutional Experiment*, with Joel A. Nichols, traces the development of civil liberties in America from the founding to the present, with a special focus on the First Amendment. The book is carefully nuanced but highly readable, a great introduction to the conversation.

My favorite read on this topic is Nicholas P. Miller, *The Religious Roots of the First Amendment.* Miller argues that long before Enlightenment philosophers like John Locke took up the case for civil liberties, dissenting Protestants in England and ultimately throughout Europe and America articulated a clear vision of the separation of church and state. It remained a minority position in Europe but became the dominant position in early America. The book is engaging and somewhat speculative but is a great introduction to the subject.

There are, of course, many more books I could recommend. This is an unsystematic list. Whatever you do, by all means continue the conversation. Commentators like to say that we live in an unprecedented age. Who can say whether Christians today face greater challenges than Backus faced in his generation? I'm inclined to believe Christians of the twenty-first century have an advantage if for no other reason than because we have examples like Backus to examine and possibly imitate. We also have a couple of centuries more hindsight than Backus had. We do well to avail ourselves of our many resources to prepare for uncertain days ahead.

ACKNOWLEDGMENTS

Many thanks to Al Hsu for his encouragement and guidance through this process. His careful work has made this book better.

A very special thanks to Amy O'Brien, my wife, who read this manuscript carefully and improved it with her insightful suggestions. More important was her support through the doctoral studies that resulted in this project. I can't thank you enough for your support.

A writer does his best to perfect a book before it goes to print. He rarely succeeds. This book has benefited from the help of many. All remaining flaws are my fault.

APPENDIX

A COMPLETE LIST OF WRITINGS BY ISAAC BACKUS

The works are listed by their full titles in alphabetical order. Italics indicates the shorter titles by which the works are more commonly known.

An Abridgment Of The Church History of New-England from 1602 to 1804. Containing A View Of Their Principles And Practices, Declensions And Revivals, Oppression And Liberty, With A Concise Account Of *The Baptists In The Southern Parts Of America* And A Chronological Table Of The Whole. Boston, 1804.

An *Address To The Inhabitants of New-England*, Concerning the present Bloody Controversy therein. Boston, 1787.

An Address To The Second Baptist Church, In Middleborough, Concerning the *Importance Of Gospel Discipline*. Middleborough, 1787.

All True Ministers of the Gospel, are called into that Work by the special Influences of the Holy Spirit. *A Discourse Showing the Nature and Necessity of an Internal Call To Preach* the Everlasting Gospel. Also Marks by which Christ's Ministers may be known from others, and Answers to sundry Objections: Together with some Observations on the Principles and Practices of many in the present Day concerning these Things. To which is added, Some short Account of the *Experiences and dying Testimony of Mr. Nathaniel Shepherd.* Boston, 1754.

An Appeal to the People Of The Massachusetts State Against Arbitrary Power. Boston, 1780.

An Appeal to the Public for Religious Liberty, Against the Oppression of the present Day. Boston, 1773.

The Atonement of Christ, Explained and Vindicated, Against Late Attempts to exclude it out of the World. Boston, 1787.

A Church History of New-England. Volume 2. Extending from 1690 to 1784. Including A concise View of the American War, and of the Conduct of the Baptists therein, with the present State of their Churches. Providence, 1784.

A Church History of New-England Extending from 1783 to 1796. Containing An Account Of The Religious Affairs Of The Country, And Of Oppressions Therein On Religious Accounts; With A Particular History Of The Baptist Churches In The Five States Of New-England. Volume 3. Boston, 1796.

Church History of New-England, from 1620 to 1804. 1804. Reprint, Philadelphia: American Baptist Publication and S. S. Society, 1844.

A Discourse, Concerning The *Materials, the Manner of Building, and Power of Organizing of the Church of Christ*; with the true Difference and exact Limits between Civil and Ecclesiastical Government; and also what are, and what are not just Reasons for Separation. Together with, An *Address to Joseph Fish*, A.M. Pastor of a Church in Stonington, occasioned by his late Piece called The Examiner Examined. Boston: John Boyles, 1773.

A Discourse Showing the Nature and Necessity of an Internal Call To Preach the Everlasting Gospel. Boston: Fowle, 1754.

The *Doctrine of Particular Election And Final Perseverance*, Explained And Vindicated. Boston: Samuel Hall, 1789.

The *Doctrine of Sovereign Grace Opened and Vindicated:* And Also The Consistency and Duty of declaring Divine Sovereignty, and Men's Impotency, while yet we address their Consciences with the Warnings of Truth, and Calls of the Gospel. Providence: John Carter, 1771.

The Doctrine Of Universal Salvation Examined and Refuted. Containing, A concise and distinct Answer to the Writings of Mr. Relly, and Mr. Winchester, upon that subject. Providence, 1782.

A Door Opened For Equal Christian Liberty, And No Man Can Shut It. This proved by plain Facts. Boston, 1783.

Evangelical Hymns and Songs; In Two Parts: The First, composed on various views of the Christian Life and Warfare; The Second, in Praise of the Redeemer. Boston, 1762.

Evangelical Ministers described, and distinguished from Legalists. A Sermon, The Substance of which was delivered October 30, 1771. At The Ordination of Mr. Asa Hunt, To the Pastoral Charge of the Third Baptist-Church in Middleborough. (Published at their request.) Boston: Philip Freeman, 1772.

Family Prayer not to be neglected. A Discourse, Wherein is Opened The Nature of Prayer in general, And the Warrant for Family Prayer in particular; With Answers to sundry Excuses for the Neglect thereof; And Address to several Sorts of Persons. Newport, Rhode Island: Samuel Hall, 1766.

A Fish caught in his own Net. An Examination of Nine Sermons, from Matt. 16.18. Published last year, by Mr. Joseph Fish of Stonington; Wherein He labours to prove that those called Standing Churches in New-England, are built upon the Rock, and upon the same Principles with the first Fathers of this Country; And that Separates and Baptists are joining with the Gates of Hell against Them. In Answer to which; Many of his Mistakes are corrected; The Constitution of those Churches opened; the Testimonies of Prophets and Apostles, and also of many of those Fathers are produced, which as plainly condemn his plan, as any Separate or Baptist can do. Boston, 1768.

Godliness Excludes Slavery. Boston: Benjamin Edes and Son, 1785.

Gospel Comfort for Mourners. A Sermon, Delivered at Middleborough, February 5, 1769, Upon Hearing Of The Death Of A Godly Mother. To Which Is Added, Some Memoirs Of Her Life. The Second Edition. With *A Short Account Of His Wife*. Boston, 1803.

Gospel Comfort, Under Heavy Tidings. The Substance Of a Sermon, delivered at Middleborough, February 5, 1769, Upon hearing of the Death of a godly Mother. To which is added, Some Memories of her Life. Providence: John Carter, 1769.

Government And Liberty Described And Ecclesiastical Tyranny Exposed. Boston, 1778.

A Great Faith described and inculcated. A Sermon On Luke VII.9. Boston, 1805.

A History of New-England. With Particular Reference to the Denomination of Christians Called Baptists. Second edition with notes by David Weston. Newton, MA: Backus Historical Society, 1871.

A History of New-England, With Particular Reference to the Denomination of Christians Called Baptists. Containing The first principles and settlements of the Country; The rise and increase of the Baptist Churches therein; The intrusion of Abritary [*sic*] Power under the cloak of Religion; The Christian Testimonies of the Baptists and others against the same, with their Sufferings under it, from the Begining [*sic*] to the present Time. Collected from most authentic Records and Writings, both Ancient and Modern. Volume 1. Boston: Edward Draper, 1777.

The Infinite Importance Of The Obedience of Faith, And Of A Separation from the World, Opened And Demonstrated. Second Edition [of True Faith will produce good Works], corrected and improved. Boston, 1791.

The Kingdom Of God, Described By His Word, With Its Infinite Benefits to Human Society. Boston, 1792.

A Letter To a Gentleman In The Massachusetts General Assembly, Concerning Taxes to support Religious Worship. N.p., 1771.

A Letter to the Reverend Mr. Benjamin Lord, of Norwich; Occasioned by some harsh Things which he has lately published against Those who have dissented from his Sentiments about the Ministry, the Church, and Baptism. Providence, Rhode Island: William Goddard, 1764.

The Liberal Support Of Gospel Ministers, Opened and Inculcated. Boston: Samuel Hall, 1790.

The *Nature and Necessity of an Internal Call To Preach* The Everlasting Gospel; With Marks to distinguish the Ministers of Christ from all Deceivers. The Second Edition Improved. Boston, 1792.

Policy, As Well As Honesty, Forbids The Use Of Secular Force In Religious Affairs. Boston, 1779.

A Reply To a Piece wrote last Year, By Mr. Israel Holly, Pastor of a Church in Suffield; Entitled "The New-Testament Interpretation of the Old, relative to Infant Baptism." Wherein Another short Attempt is made toward bringing that Controversy to a happy issue. Newport: Solomon Southwick, 1772.

A Seasonable Please for Liberty of Conscience, Against Some Late Oppressive Proceedings; Particularly in the Town of Berwick, In the County of York. Boston: Philip Freeman, 1770.

A Short Description of the difference between the *Bond-Woman and the Free*; As they are the two Covenants, with the Characters and Conditions of each of their Children: Considered in a Sermon Delivered at Middleborough, Wherein is particularly shewn, that none are proper Subjects of the special Ordinances of the Gospel-Church, but real Saints. Boston, 1756.

A Short Description Of the difference Between the *Bond-Woman and the Free*, As they are the Two Covenants. With the Characters and Condition of each of their Children. The Second Edition corrected. To which is now added, *An Answer To Mr. Frothingham's late Letter*, concerning Baptism. Boston, 1770.

The Sovereign Decrees of God, Set In A Scriptural Light, And Vindicated against the Blasphemy contained in a late Paper, entitled, On Traditionary Zeal. In a Letter to a Friend. Boston, 1773.

Spiritual Ignorance causeth Men to Counter-act their Doctrinal Knowledge. A Discourse From Acts xiii.27. Providence, [New England]: William Goddard, 1763.

The Substance of an *Address to an Assembly in Bridgewater*, March 10, 1779, Previous to the Administration of Baptism. Providence, Rhode Island: John Carter, 1779.

The *Testimony Of The Two Witnesses*, Explained And Improved. Providence, 1786.

The *Testimony Of The Two Witnesses*, Explained And Vindicated, With A Few *Remarks Upon The Late Writings of Dr. Hemmenway And Dr. Lathrop*. The Second Edition, improved. Boston, 1793.

True Faith will produce good Works. A Discourse Wherein are opened The Nature of Faith, and its powerful Influence on the Heart and Life; together with the contrary Nature and Effects of Unbelief: And Answers to various Objections. To which are Perfixed [*sic*] A brief View of the *present State of the Protestant World*, with some Remarks on the *Writings of Mr. Sandeman*. Boston: D. Kneeland, 1767.

Truth Is Great, And Will Prevail. Boston, 1781.

NOTES

Introduction

2 *a "wall of separation"*: Thomas Jefferson, "Jefferson's Letter to the Danbury Baptists," January 1, 1802, www.loc.gov/loc/lcib/9806/danpre.html.

3 *long-standing American tradition of accommodating religious practice*: Jay Alan Sekulow, "Religious Liberty and Expression Under Attack: Restoring America's First Freedoms," Heritage Foundation, October 1, 2012, www.heritage.org/civil-society/report/religious-liberty-and-expression-under-attack-restoring-americas-first.

4 *set forth the principles of separation of Church and State*: William McLoughlin, *Isaac Backus and the American Pietistic Tradition*, ed. Oscar Handlin, Library of American Biography (Boston: Little, Brown, 1967), xi.

6 *Nothing teaches like experience*: Isaac Backus, *A History of New-England, With Particular Reference to the Denomination of Christians Called Baptists*, ed. David Weston, 2nd ed. (Newton, MA: Backus Historical Society, 1871), vii.

9 *He was a burning and shining light*: Thomas Baldwin, quoted in Alvah Hovey, *A Memoir of the Life and Times of the Rev. Isaac Backus* (Boston: Gould & Lincoln, 1858), 311-12.

a "young upstart, not to be regarded": Isaac Backus, "A Fish Caught in His Own Net," in *Isaac Backus on Church, State, and Calvinism: Pamphlets, 1754–1789*, ed. William McLoughlin (Cambridge, MA: Belknap Press, 1968), 178.

10 *the American public was almost evenly divided*: David Masci, "Key Findings About Americans' Views on Religious Liberty and Nondiscrimination," Pew Research Center, September 28, 2016, www.pewresearch.org/fact-tank/2016/09/28/key-findings-about-americans-views-on-religious-liberty-and-nondiscrimination.

12 *The goal of this book*: I wrote a doctoral dissertation on this aspect of Backus. See Brandon J. O'Brien, "The Edwardsean Isaac Backus: The Significance of Jonathan Edwards in Backus's Theology, History, and Defense of Religious Liberty" (PhD diss., Trinity Evangelical Divinity School, 2013). There are essentially three biographies about Backus: Hovey, *Memoir*; T. B. Maston, *Isaac Backus: Pioneer of Religious Liberty* (Rochester, NY: American Baptist Historical Society, 1963); and McLoughlin, *Isaac Backus and the American Pietistic Tradition.*

Chapter 1: "Filled Up with Sin"

17 *New England's beauties, which still seemed to me*: Benjamin Tompson, *New England's Crisis* (Boston: John Foster, 1676).

Frequent bloody conflicts with Native Americans: For more on this see Francis J. Bremer, *The Puritan Experiment: New England Society from Bradford to Edwards* (Lebanon, NH: University Press of New England, 1995), 154-67.

18 *congregations experienced seasons of spiritual revival*: Thomas Kidd offers a helpful discussion of covenant renewal services, especially as precursors to the Great Awakening, in *The Great Awakening: The Roots of Evangelical Christianity in Colonial America* (New Haven, CT: Yale University Press, 2007), 3-5.

19 *only 17 percent of American colonists were religiously affiliated*: Roger Finke and Rodney Stark, *The Churching of America, 1776–2005: Winners and Losers in Our Religious Economy* (New Brunswick, NJ: Rutgers University Press, 2006), 29. The percentage would almost certainly have been smaller in the decades before the Great Awakening of the 1740s.

well-developed youth culture: George M. Marsden, *A Short Life of Jonathan Edwards* (Grand Rapids: Eerdmans, 2008), 43-44.

a third of babies were conceived out of wedlock: Finke and Stark, *Churching of America*, 25.

20 *an excellent piece of music*: Benjamin Franklin, *The Autobiography of Benjamin Franklin* (New York: Walter J. Black, 1941), 168.

He had a loud and clear voice: ibid., 167-68.

21 *the entire populations of Boston and Philadelphia*: "Top 20 U.S. Metropolitan Areas by Population, 1790-2010," Peakbagger.com, www.peakbagger.com/PBGeog/histmetropop.aspx#tables.

Nathan Cole's experience of hearing Whitefield preach: Nathan Cole, quoted in George Leon Walker, *Some Aspects of the Religious Life of New England* (New York: Silver, Burdett, 1897), 89-92.

23-24 *Franklin's observations of hearing Whitefield preach*: Franklin, *Autobiography*, 164.

25 *average church attendance in Edwards's day*: Finke and Stark, *Churching of America*, 29.

27 *As I was mowing in the field alone*: Isaac Backus, *The Diary of Isaac Backus*, ed. William G. McLoughlin, vol. 3, 1786–1806 (Providence, RI: Brown University Press, 1979), 1525.

28 *marks of true grace*: ibid., 1526.

29 *book-burning populists*: See Kidd's *Great Awakening* for a thorough introduction to the full cast of characters in this interesting story.

30 *James Davenport arrested for slander*: Backus heard James Davenport preach in Norwich in 1741. See Backus, *Diary of Isaac Backus*, 3:1523-24.

32 *percentage of Congregationalists in New England and Norwich, CT*: Finke and Stark, *Churching of America*, 44.

33 *Standing Order*: This was the term often used to describe Congregational clergy. Congregational ministers were privileged and socially elite, and the term "Standing Order" connoted their special status in New England culture.

Pew Religious Landscape Study: Religious Landscape Study, Pew Research Center, www.pewforum.org/religious-landscape-study.

Chapter 2: Ministry and the Holy Spirit

35 *the world behind me, the cross before me*: Attributed to Sadhu Sundar Singh, "I Have Decided to Follow Jesus," n.d.

36 *the beginning of the democratization of American Christianity*: This phrase is borrowed from Nathan O. Hatch, *The Democratization of American Christianity* (New Haven, CT: Yale University Press, 1991).

Chauncey's view of the New Lights: Charles Chauncy, "Seasonable Thoughts on the State of Religion in New England," *Evans Early American Imprint Collection*, accessed October 10, 2017, http://quod.lib.umich.edu/e/evans/N04182.0001.001/1:2?rgn=div1;view=fulltext.

39 *Lord's Supper leading to personal conversion*: Solomon Stoddard, grandfather of Jonathan Edwards, considered the Lord's Supper a "converting ordinance"—a practice that might lead someone to faith. For a fascinating insight into the nature of this debate, see Edward Taylor, *Edward Taylor vs. Solomon Stoddard: The Nature of the Lord's Supper*, The Unpublished Writings of Edward Taylor, vol. 2 (Boston: Twayne, 1981).

40 *though they had a form of godliness*: Isaac Backus, *The Diary of Isaac Backus*, ed. William G. McLoughlin, vol. 1, *1741–1764* (Providence, RI: Brown University Press, 1979), 3.

42 *Backus and friends met together in one another's homes*: ibid.

that the gifts that he had given me, did belong to the church: ibid., 4.

43 *the hand of the Lord was powerfully upon me*: ibid.

God "spoke them words with power to my soul": ibid.

45 *Though it was extraordinary bad traveling*: ibid., 15.

46 *I desire to be humbled by God*: ibid., 32.

48 *I was led to view a large field all white to harvest here*: ibid., 12.

49 *He didn't grant them authority to affirm or deny his call*: ibid., 18.

By the summer of 1748: Isaac Backus, *The Diary of Isaac Backus*, ed. William G. McLoughlin, vol. 1, 1741-1764 (Providence: Brown University Press, 1979), 75.

50 *our minds appeared to harmonize in the design*: ibid., 75.

Jesus and his disciples were at the wedding: Isaac Backus, quoted in Alvah Hovey, *A Memoir of the Life and Times of the Rev. Isaac Backus* (Boston: Gould & Lincoln, 1858), 81.

51 *Backus called Susanna*: Alvah Hovey, *A Memoir of the Life and Times of the Rev. Isaac Backus* (Boston: Gould & Lincoln, 1858), 39.

what the Lord had done for their souls: Backus, *Diary of Isaac Backus*, 1:31.

Chapter 3: Becoming Baptist

55 *Seventeenth-century Baptists were Arminian in theology*: Like all issues in this time period, the doctrinal diversity among seventeenth-century Baptists is a complicated matter. For a helpful introduction to this discussion, see chapter four of David W. Bebbington, *Baptists Through the Centuries: A History of a Global People* (Waco, TX: Baylor University Press, 2010).

56 *court statement about Baptists*: William McLoughlin, *Isaac Backus and the American Pietist Tradition*, ed. Oscar Handlin, Library of American Biography (Boston: Little, Brown, 1967), 58.

57 *I hear you have been dipped to wash away your taxes*: ibid., 60.

60 *the status of those "who have been baptized and yet are not believers"*: Alvah Hovey, *A Memoir of the Life and Times of the Rev. Isaac Backus* (Boston: Gould & Lincoln, 1858), 87.

61 *particularly fine dressing*: Isaac Backus, *The Diary of Isaac Backus*, ed. William G. McLoughlin, vol. 1, *1741–1764* (Providence, RI: Brown University Press, 1979), 59.

62 *I have been under great trials*: ibid., 61.

Alas! I had but a poor ending of the year: ibid., 119.

64 *No man who has not experienced the like*: Hovey, *Memoir*, 90.

a day of secret fasting and prayer: ibid., 91.

70 *they esteem such church to be one of their denomination*: McLoughlin, *Isaac Backus and the American Pietist Tradition*, 114.

Chapter 4: No More "Nursing Fathers"

73 *Trinity Lutheran Church Child Learning Center*: Trinity Lutheran Church of Columbia, Inc. v. Comer, Director, Missouri Department of Natural Resources, 582 U. S. ____ (2017), www.supremecourt.gov/opinions/16pdf/15-577_khlp.pdf.

77 *Civil rulers ought to be nursing fathers to the church*: Edward Dorr, "The Duty of Civil Magistrates to Be Nursing Fathers to the Church of Christ" (Hartford, CT: Thomas Greene, 1765), 7; emphasis added.

Civil government is obliged to promote religion through taxation: ibid., 10. The imperative force of Isaiah 49:23 is also explicit in Calvin's letters to monarchs that preface English the editions of his *Commentary on Psalms*. In his prefatory letter to the Protestant king Edward VI ("a truly Christian prince"), Calvin implies that the duty placed on rulers in Isaiah 49:23 constitutes the central theme of the entire book, at least for a ruling monarch. According to Calvin, "God himself addresses you [Edward] by the mouth of his servant Isaiah, charging you to proceed, to the utmost of your ability and power, in carrying forward the restoration of the church." "More especially," he continues, "Isaiah . . . *calls Kings the nursing fathers of the Church*, (Is. xlix. 23) and does not permit them to withhold that assistance which her afflicted condition demands." Likewise, when Elizabeth became queen of England, Calvin enjoined her to remember that "the Prophet Isaiah demands not only from *Kings* that they be *nursingfathers*, but also from *Queens* that they be *nursingmothers*." John Calvin, *Commentary on the Book of the Prophet Isaiah*, vol. 1 (Grand Rapids: Baker Books, 1999), xxiv, xviii.

78 *a time when formerly hostile forces acknowledge Christ as true God*: John Calvin says simply that "the prophecy refers to the advent of Christ." See Calvin's *Institutes of the Christian Religion*, rev. ed. (Peabody, MA: Hendrickson, 2007), 5.20.5.

Constantine "not only submitted to the yoke of Christ": John Calvin, *Commentary on Isaiah*, trans. William Pringle (Edinburgh: T. Constable, 1852), 4:39-40.

Hence it ought to be observed that something remarkable: ibid., 40.

79 *removing superstitions and putting an end to all wicked idolatry*: ibid.

Undoubtedly, while kings bestow careful attention: ibid., 40-41.

The twofold duty Calvin outlines for monarchs: The barrenness of Israel and the desolation of Jerusalem are recurring metaphors for God's judgment of the nation in Isaiah 40-54. Isaiah 49:17-18 brings together the two themes of rebuilding the walls of Zion and repopulating the city with children returned from exile. "The new note sounded [in vv. 22-23] turns on the role of the nations in bringing back Zion's sons and daughters, of course, now in their function as servants and slaves." That is, the foreign monarchs cease to be monarchs and assume the domestic position of nursemaids. Beyond this, Isaiah does not prescribe what "nursing fathers" would do. Neither do modern commentators elaborate on the image. Brevard Childs, *Isaiah*. The Old Testament Library (Louisville: Westminster John Knox, 2001), 392.

80 *holy kings are especially praised for restoring worship of God*: Calvin, *Institutes of the Christian Religion*, 4.20.9.

the magistrate is to see that the ministry be duly provided for: "Of the Maintenance of Church Officers," The Cambridge Platform 11.4, accessed October 10, 2017, www.archive.org/stream/cambridgeplatfo00goog/cambridgeplatfo00goog_djvu.txt. Emphasis added.

81 *when a good and religious prince ascended the throne of Israel*: Dorr, "Duty of Civil Magistrates," 14.

when Moses and Aaron walk hand in hand: ibid., 32.

82 *Mrs. Backus would not abandon her religious principles*: Alvah Hovey, *A Memoir of the Life and Times of the Rev. Isaac Backus* (Boston: Gould & Lincoln, 1858), 29-30.

Backus's first tract: Isaac Backus, *A Discourse Showing the Nature and Necessity of an Internal Call to Preach the Everlasting Gospel* (Boston: Fowle, 1754). This is cited in William G. McLoughlin, *Isaac Backus on Church, State, and Calvinism: Pamphlets, 1754-1789* (Cambridge, MA: Harvard University Press, 1968), 70.

83 *Multitudes place their qualifications more in human learning*: ibid., 75.

And yet the essence and nature of conversion: ibid., 79.

What was spoken to any of God's people of old: ibid., 77.

84 *Backus's 1756 pamphlet*: Isaac Backus, *A Short Description of the Difference Between the Bond-Woman and the Free* (Boston: Green & Russell, 1756), cited in McLoughlin, *Isaac Backus on Church, State, and Calvinism*, 65-128.

85 *Old Testament as a covenant of works*: ibid., 137.

New Testament as a covenant of grace: ibid., 139.

86 *The promises and threatenings of the old covenant*: ibid., 145; emphasis added.

87 *the new covenant and the relationship of church and state*: For more on the use of the "nursing fathers" metaphor and what it indicates about hermeneutic principles in the Reformed tradition, see James H. Hutson, "'Nursing Fathers': The Model for Church-State Relations in America from James I to Jefferson," in *Lectures on Religion and the Founding of the American Republic*, ed. John W. Welch (Provo, UT: Brigham Young University Press, 2003), 7-24. For a brief introduction to the mode of hermeneutics employed by the Anabaptists and early Baptists, see John H. Yoder, "The Hermeneutics of the Anabaptists," in *Essays on Biblical Interpretations: Anabaptist-Mennonite Perspectives*, ed. Willard Swartley (Elkhart, IN: Institute of Mennonite Studies, 1984).

Israel Holly wrote two tracts in response to Backus's hermeneutical writings. See Israel Holly, *The New Testament Interpretation of the Old . . . Written Letter-wise to Mr. Isaac Backus, Occasioned by His Late Answer to Mr. F——'s Letter in Favour of Infant Baptism* (New London, CT: T. Green, 1771); and *A Second Letter to Mr. Isaac Backus: Upon the Controversy Concerning the Proper Subjects of Baptism* (Hartford, CT: Eben. Watson, 1774). Backus responded to the first letter. Isaac Backus, *A Reply to a Piece Wrote Last Year by Mr. Israel Holly* (Newport, RI: Solomon Southwick, 1772).

88 *Carter and Robertson aspire to political influence*: See D. Michael Lindsay, *Faith in the Halls of Power: How Evangelicals Joined the American Elite* (New York: Oxford University Press, 2007), 15-16.

89 *Ronald Reagan sympathetic to evangelical causes*: Kenneth J. Collins, *Power, Politics and the Fragmentation of Evangelicalism: From the Scopes Trial to the Obama Administration* (Downers Grove, IL: IVP Academic, 2012), 106; and Lindsay, *Faith in the Halls of Power*, 18-20.

Christians and non-Christians view this waning influence in different ways: Robert P. Jones et al., "How Immigration and Concerns About Cultural Changes Are Shaping the 2016 Election: Findings from the 2016 PRRI/Brookings Immigration Survey" (Public Religion Research Institute, June 23, 2016), 17.

Chapter 5: A Record of Wrongs

94 *the art of disputing against the truth*: Isaac Backus, "A Fish Caught in His Own Net," in *Isaac Backus on Church, State, and Calvinism: Pamphlets, 1754-17809*, ed. William G. McLoughlin (Cambridge, MA: Belknap Press, 1968), 209.

many scholars that have come out of college of late are rank Arminians: Isaac Backus, *A Discourse Showing the Nature and Necessity of an Internal Call to Preach the Everlasting Gospel* (Boston: Fowle, 1754), cited in McLoughlin, *Isaac Backus on Church, State, and Calvinism*, 74.

95 *covenanted before God to embrace further light*: Backus, "Fish Caught in His Own Net," 262. A later chapter is dedicated to Backus's view of history and his conviction that Baptists were the true heirs of the reforming vision of the founding fathers. Included in that discussion is more on Backus's complex understanding of the authority of the fathers.

97 *Abraham sensed a general "spirit of opposition against the Spirit of God in the church"*: Abraham Lord, quoted in Backus, *A Seasonable Plea for Liberty of Conscience* (Boston: Freeman, 1770), 4.

nothing but very weighty and grievous things lying upon the conscience: ibid., 5.

98 *Liberty of conscience we claim ourselves and allow others as a darling point*: ibid., 42.

If it is only the church that is to judge: ibid., 5; emphasis added.

100 *when we have delivered our sentiments and the grounds of them*: Isaac Backus, *True Faith Will Produce Good Works*, cited in McLoughlin, *Isaac Backus on Church, State, and Calvinism*, 90.

for the secular arm to finish what the church has begun: ibid.

The church has declared the Baptist to be irregular: Backus, *Seasonable Plea*, 8.

101 *It is not the pence but the power, that alarms us*: Isaac Backus, quoted in Alvah Hovey, *A Memoir of the Life and Times of the Rev. Isaac Backus* (Boston: Gould & Lincoln, 1858), 236.

103 *confiscated Baptist property sold for "nineteen pounds three shillings"*: ibid., 178.

103 *destruction of an apple orchard*: William McLoughlin, *Isaac Backus and the American Pietist Tradition*, ed. Oscar Handlin, Library of American Biography (Boston: Little, Brown, 1967), 117.

104 *Baptist advertisement in a Boston newspaper*: Hovey, *Memoir*, 175.

109 *well-attested evidence of abuse suffered by Baptists*: ibid.

107 *Martha Kimball's story of injustice*: ibid., 185.

Chapter 6: Religious Liberty on the Eve of War

113 *offer a few thoughts concerning the general nature of liberty and government*: Isaac Backus, *An Appeal to the Public for Religious Liberty*, in *Isaac Backus on Church, State, and Calvinism: Pamphlets, 1754-17809*, ed. William G. McLoughlin (Cambridge, MA: Belknap Press, 1968), 309.

114 *Backus's definition of "true human liberty"*: ibid.

submission to government and acting strictly by rule was confinement: ibid., 310.

The first humans followed "the authority of Heaven": ibid.

Man first lost his freedom by breaking over the rules of government: ibid., 309.

the social consequences of this rebellion: ibid., 310.

114-15 *Ever since Adam sinned*: Isaac Backus, *An Appeal to the Public for Religious Liberty, Against the Oppressions of the Present Day* (Boston: 1773).

116 *'tis only the power of the Gospel that can set them free from sin*: ibid., 311-12.

117 *infant baptism laid the foundation of a national church*: Isaac Backus, "A Letter to the Reverend Mr. Benjamin Lord, of Norwich; Occasioned by some harsh Things which he has lately published against Those who have dissented from his Sentiments about the Ministry, the Church, and Baptism" (Providence, RI: William Goddard, 1764), 18.

infant baptism is never expressed in the Bible: Backus, *Appeal to the Public*, 317.

Backus's writing about clergy selection: Baptism and clergy requirements were the issues Backus addressed first in print. A good place to start is with these two tracts, both available in William McLoughlin, ed.,

Isaac Backus on Church, State, and Calvinism: Pamphlets, 1754–1789 (Cambridge, MA: Belknap Press, 1968); Isaac Backus, *A Discourse Showing the Nature and Necessity of an Internal Call to Preach the Everlasting Gospel* (Boston: Fowle, 1754); and Backus, *A Short Description of the Difference Between the Bond-Woman and the Free* (Boston: Green & Russell, 1756).

117 *must be one who has either an academical [*sic*] degree*: Backus, *Appeal to the Public*, 317.

Backus's use of 1 Corinthians 9:13-14 and Galatians 6:6-7: ibid., 318.

the ministers of our land have chosen to live by the law: ibid., 320. For a full exposition of Backus's position see Isaac Backus, "A Fish Caught in His Own Net," in McLoughlin, *Isaac Backus on Church, State, and Calvinism*, 237-43.

119 *it is against the interest of the people we apply to, to grant us any remedy*: Isaac Backus, quoted in Alvah Hovey, *A Memoir of the Life and Times of the Rev. Isaac Backus* (Boston: Gould & Lincoln, 1858), 223. Thus at the heart of Backus's rejection of establishment in New England was an Edwardsean understanding of the operations of the human will.

120 *the majority of the people the test of orthodoxy*: Backus, *Appeal to the Public*, 321.

the grand test of their orthodoxy is the major vote of the people: ibid., 318.

The grand contest ever since sin entered into the world: Isaac Backus, *The Sovereign Decrees of God* (1773), in McLoughlin, *Isaac Backus on Church, State, and Calvinism*, 295.

121 *It may now be asked—What is the liberty desired?*: Hovey, *Memoir*, 210.

The delegates from Massachusetts used all their arts: ibid.

The delegates' responses to Backus: ibid., 211.

123 *The presentation had been presented to outsiders*: For a fuller discussion of the different worldviews vying for dominance at this time in history, see George M. Marsden, *Religion and American Culture*, 2nd ed. (Belmont, CA: Wadsworth, 2001), 38-56.

124 *John Hancock, president of the Congress*: Isaac Backus, *A History of New-England, With particular Reference to the Denomination of Christians called Baptists*, 2nd ed. (Newton, MA: Backus Historical Society, 1871), 549.

See also *The* Journals of each Provincial Congress of Massachusetts in 1774 and 1775, and of the Committee of Safety (Boston: Dutton and Wentworth, 1838), 67.

Chapter 7: New Liberties in the New World

126 *Backus's massive three-volume narrative:* The volume was published in 1777: *A History of New-England*, vol. 1 (Boston: Edward Draper, 1777). A second volume followed in 1784: *A Church History of New-England*, vol. 2 (Providence: 1784). The final volume appeared in 1796: *A Church History of New-England*, vol. 3 (Boston, 1796).

127 *danger of allowing the Baptist message to spread*: For a helpful discussion about the historical relationship between Anabaptists and Baptists, see David W. Bebbington, *Baptists Through the Centuries: A History of a Global People* (Waco, TX: Baylor University Press, 2010), 25-41.

129 *Puritans and Pilgrims had different view of religious liberty*: See, for example, David Hackett Fischer, *Albion's Seed: Four British Folkways in America* (New York: Oxford University Press, 1989).

132 *He shall make us a praise and glory*: The full text of John Winthrop's 1630 sermon, "A Model of Christian Charity" is available online at the Winthrop Society website: www.winthropsociety.com/doc_charity.php.

133 *Quakers ears cut off*: Alvah Hovey, *A Memoir of the Life and Times of the Rev. Isaac Backus* (Boston: Gould & Lincoln, 1858), 164.

134 *Williams accepted as "of good account in England for a godly preacher"*: Backus, *History of New-England*, 1:39.

137 *Hovey's understanding of Backus's motivation*: Hovey, *Memoir*, 24-25.

139 *The heritage of religious liberty in America extends to the Reformation*: See Barry Alan Shain, *The Myth of American Individualism: The Protestant Origins of American Political Thought* (Princeton, NJ: Princeton University Press, 1994); and Nicolas P. Miller, *The Religious Roots of the First Amendment: Dissenting Protestants and the Separation of Church and State* (New York: Oxford University Press, 2012).

legal historians are forceful advocates of this thesis: See Peter Judson Richards, "A Clear and Steady Channel": Isaac Backus and the Limits of Liberty," *Journal of Church and State* 43, no. 3 (summer 2001):

447-82; see especially John Witte Jr., "The Theology and Politics of the First Amendment Religion Clauses: A Bicentennial Essay," *Emory Law Journal* 40 (1991): 490-507; John Witte Jr., *Religion and the American Constitutional Experiment: Essential Rights and Liberties* (Boulder, CO: Westview Press, 2000); John Witte Jr., "Facts and Fictions About the History of Separation of Church and State," *Journal of Church and State* 48, no. 1 (2006): 14-45; and John Witte Jr., *The Reformation of Rights: Law, Religion, and Human Rights in Early Modern Calvinism* (New York: Cambridge University Press, 2007).

140 *a new history of Western rights*: Witte, *Reformation of Rights*, 20, 2.

Disestablishment "was a populist movement": Nicholas P. Miller, *The Religious Roots of the First Amendment: Dissenting Protestants and the Separation of Church and State* (New York: Oxford University Press, 2012), 4. See also Chris Beneke, *Beyond Toleration: The Religious Origins of American Pluralism* (Oxford: Oxford University Press, 2006); and William R. Estep, *The Revolution Within the Revolution: The First Amendment in Historical Context, 1612–1789* (Grand Rapids: Eerdmans, 1990).

Chapter 8: Backus, Baptists, and the Bill of Rights

144 *the "obnoxious principle" of state taxation was preserved in the draft*: Isaac Backus, quoted in Alvah Hovey, *A Memoir of the Life and Times of the Rev. Isaac Backus* (Boston: Gould & Lincoln, 1858), 238.

145 *All men are born equally free*: Isaac Backus, "A Declaration of the Rights, of the Inhabitants of the State of Massachusetts-Bay, in New-England," 1779, in *The Diary of Isaac Backus*, ed. William G. McLoughlin, vol. 3, *1786–1806* (Providence, RI: Brown University Press, 1979). The language borrows extensively from the language of the Virginia bill of rights that was adopted in 1776, with significant changes that reflect Backus's unique theology and philosophy.

148 *a false memorial of grievances, in order to break the union of these colonies*: Backus, quoted in Hovey, *Memoir*, 238.

149 *Backus's "tract to publicize the accusation and denounce it"*: ibid., 239.

Our churches are built upon the law: ibid., 240.

150 *not a shadow of right in the general government to intermeddle with religion*: James Madison, quoted in John Witte Jr. and Joel A. Nichols,

Religion and the American Constitutional Experiment, 4th ed. (New York: Oxford University Press, 2016), 70.

150 *A bill of rights is neither an essential nor a necessary instrument*: James Wilson, quoted in ibid., 70.

152 *Madison, if asked, would likely give credit to John Leland*: Joe L. Coker, "Sweet Harmony vs Strict Separation: Recognizing the Distinction between Isaac Backus and John Leland," *American Baptist Quarterly* 16, no. 3 (summer 1997): 244. See Leon H. McBeth, *The Baptist Heritage: Four Centuries of Baptist Witness* (Nashville: B&H Academic, 1987), 282-83. The Library of Congress has a copy of a friendly letter from Leland to Madison congratulating the latter for his appointment as representative (1789). Leland refers to Madison as a "particular friend," and says he wrote in case he should not be home when Madison drops by Leland's house on his way to Congress. See a copy of the letter at the Library of Congress website: http://memory.loc.gov/master/mss/mjm/03/0900/0940d.jpg.

153 *a door is now opened, for the establishment of righteous government*: Backus, *Diary of Isaac Backus*, 3:1220.

each state is at liberty now to abolish slavery as soon as they please: ibid.

155 *The greatest journey I ever went*: ibid., 1273-74.

Indeed, if elegance of style and composition were necessary: Isaac Backus, quoted in Alvah Hovey, *A Memoir of the Life and Times of the Rev. Isaac Backus* (Boston: Gould & Lincoln, 1858), 251.

From 1790 to 1797 he annually rode over 1,100 miles on horseback: McLoughlin, *Isaac Backus and the American Pietistic Tradition*, ed. Oscar Handlin, Library of American Biography (Boston: Little, Brown, 1967), 223.

156 *the first Baptist periodical in America*: ibid., 214.

157 *Susanna "expired without any great struggles"*: Backus, *Diary of Isaac Backus*, 3:1462.

The change in my family is unspeakably great: ibid., 1463.

Backus "noted sadly that only fourteen persons were still alive": McLoughlin, *Isaac Backus and the American Pietistic Tradition*, 224.

158 *Although stupidity has greatly prevailed*: Isaac Backus, *The Diary of Isaac Backus*, ed. William G. McLoughlin, vol. 3, 1786-1806 (Providence: Brown University Press, 1979), 1473.

According to the best accounts: ibid.

159 *it was as agreeable [a] meeting as I ever had*: Backus, *Diary of Isaac Backus*, 3:1514.

Mr. Backus was called "Father": William G. McLoughlin, *Isaac Backus and the American Pietistic Tradition*, ed. Oscar Handlin, Library of American Biography (Boston: Little, Brown, 1967), 230.

160 *Backus's "almost perfect embodiment of the evangelical spirit of his times"*: McLoughlin, *Isaac Backus and the American Pietistic Tradition*, 230.

Chapter 9: Where to Go from Here

164 *avoid evil ways; especially to guard against all cruelty*: Isaac Backus, *Church History of New England, from 1620 to 1804* (Philadelphia: American Baptist Publication and S. S. Society, 1844), 18.

GENERAL INDEX

OTHER BOOKS BY BRANDON J. O'BRIEN

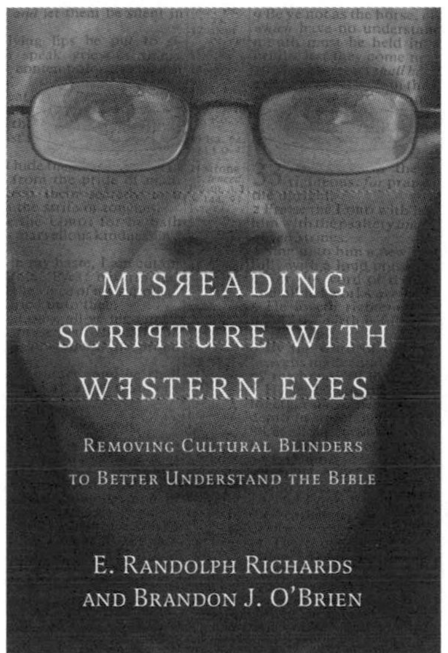

Misreading Scripture with Western Eyes
978-0-8308-3782-3

Paul Behaving Badly
978-0-8308-4472-2